UNSTOPPABLE INCREASE

RICHARD ROBERTS

UNSTOPPABLE INCREASE

Keys to Unlocking the Abundant Life God Has for You

RICHARD ROBERTS
ORAL ROBERTS MINISTRIES

Published by Oral Roberts Evangelistic Association
P.O. Box 2187
Tulsa, OK 74102
SKU 2537

Printed in the United States of America.

ISBN 978-0-9746756-9-5

Table of Contents

Foreword

Why I'm Writing this Book

Do you need increase in your life?

Do you need an increase in your finances? How about an increase in your family, business or job? Or perhaps you need an increase in your health, or in some other area of your life.

Many of you have faced difficulties, and those difficulties have led to what looks like decrease instead of increase. Others of you have walked down what you might call a dangerous path, and Satan is fighting you right now. Maybe you have been through some sort of wilderness experience and you've wondered, *where is God in all this?*

I'm here to tell you, *God is not to blame.*

Yes, there is a real devil out there. And according to John 10:10, he is working overtime to steal, kill and destroy. But that scripture also says that Jesus is present in your life too, and He has come so you could have life...abundant life...life that is overflowing with provision and filled with increase in every area...spirit, soul and body.

Friend, there is a future for you! Jeremiah 29:11 tells us God has a plan for you, and it's a good plan! It's not His plan for you to end up stuck in a ditch or forced down a dangerous path. It's not His plan for you to be hopelessly in debt or have areas of your life that are lacking in His blessings.

In fact, the Lord spoke to me about this. He told me there is a new season coming for God's people. A new season of abundance is coming.

But it's coming only into the lives of people who are willing to do what He has instructed us to do in His Word. You see, He's an "if-then" God. His promises are based on our obedience to Him. *If* we believe in our hearts and confess with our mouths that He is Lord, *then* we shall be saved. *If* we ask, seek and knock, *then* we find, and the door is opened to us. *If* we speak to our mountain of challenges and troubles in faith, *then* He moves the mountain out of our way.

In other words, when we want to see God move in our lives, we have to do something first. Then — and only then — He will do His part. He promises us salvation, healing, provision, restoration, wisdom and increase...but only if we believe, receive, confess, obey and give to Him in faith believing for our harvests. Only He can do what He can do. But only you and I can do what we can do.

I'll say it again. There's a new season coming. In fact, I believe with all my heart that God *wants* you to have a new season of abundance. But it's only coming to those who do their part, so that He can do His part.

You may be asking, *Richard, what does that mean to me? What is my part when it comes to walking in unstoppable increase in my life?*

That's what this book is all about.

Chapter 1

The God Kind of Increase

Behold I have opened a door for you. I have set open a door for you, and no man will be able to close it.

— Revelation 3:8

I believe the message in this book is one of the most important messages that God has ever given me to share with the Body of Christ. And it came to me in a most unusual way. Here is what happened.

I'm usually up very early in the morning. I wake up about 4 or 5 o'clock, roll out of bed, put on my robe, and head into the den in our home. I have a big comfortable chair in the den, where I have my prayer time in the morning.

On this particular morning, it was about 5 o'clock when I arose and sat on the edge of the bed. I'm sure you know what that's like; you sit on the edge of the bed for a minute before you get up. Well, I was rubbing my eyes, just trying to get myself awake, when clear as a bell, just as clear as I've ever heard the Lord, I heard Him say this to me:

"I'm bringing seven new seasons into the life of those who will sow."

I stopped rubbing my eyes and I said, "Lord, what was that?"

And He said to me again, "I'm bringing seven new seasons into the life of those who will sow." While I was taking that in, I heard Him say, "But to those who will not sow, I'm not going to bring those seven seasons, and they will never know it. Their life will just continue to rock along as it has been, and many of them will say, 'Why God? Why has all this happened to me? Why aren't you dealing with me?'"

You see, I believe the Lord is doing something special in the lives of those who will sow in faith to Him. He said, "I'm bringing seven new seasons into the life of the sower." I believe those of us who get on board with where He is going…those of us who commit to doing things His way…will see His increase coming into our lives more and more.

What Does the God Kind of Increase Look Like?

In Deuteronomy 28, the Lord promises His people a great blessing. Verses 1 and 2 say this:

Now it shall come to pass, if you diligently obey the voice of the Lord your God, to observe carefully all His commandments which I command you today, that the Lord your God will set you high above all nations of the earth. And all these blessings shall come upon you and overtake you, because you obey the voice of the Lord your God.

God says that this Deuteronomy 28 blessing, which covers every area of living — spirit, soul and body — comes into the lives of all those who diligently obey His voice and follow His commandments. I encourage you to read the entire chapter to see the full description of these blessings, but let me share with you briefly what God promises to you as you obey Him:

- You will be blessed in the city and blessed in the country, wherever you live and wherever you travel (v. 3).
- Your children will be blessed (v. 4).
- Your crops and livestock — in other words, your business and job, the things that bring in income — will be blessed (v. 4).
- Your basket and kneading trough — your personal resources — will be blessed (v. 5).
- You will be blessed when you come in and blessed when you go out (v. 6).
- God will defeat your enemy, the devil, when he comes against you (v. 7).
- God will bless everything you set your hand to do. And the land (or anything) He gives you, He'll bless (v. 8).
- As you obey Him, He'll bless you as His child (v. 9).
- You'll be blessed with abundant prosperity (v. 11).
- You'll be free from the bondage of debt (v. 12).
- You'll be on top of life, not at the bottom (v. 13).

That's a pretty impressive list of blessings, isn't it? This is what increase looks like to God. It's blessing upon blessing in every area where you might have a need. It's rising to the top in any situation you may face. It's not just knowing that

God is a good God...but actually seeing and experiencing His goodness all day long, no matter what is going on in your circumstances.

What God Gives, We Must Receive

Yes, God has a long list of blessings that He desires to bestow upon His children. But I want you to understand this essential key to *receiving* those blessings, because they don't come to you automatically, any more than money grows on trees. To get yourself into position to receive what He has for you, you must do something first.

You see, we serve a God whose promises to us are mostly conditional. I like to say He's an *if-then* God. Before He can fulfill His part, we have to do something first. Only He can do what He can do, but only you and I can do what we can do. In other words, without Him I cannot, but without me He will not.

The good news is, you and God *together in partnership* can accomplish some amazing things in life. Believe me, even though He asks us to do something first — to act on our faith — He's not doing it out of ill will or judgment or a desire to control us. No, the things He asks us to do are *for our benefit*! He wants to lead us along His paths, so that we can enjoy His safety, His protection and His provision.

Jeremiah 29:11 tells us God has a plan for you, and it's a good plan! It's not His plan for you to be in a ditch or walk down a dangerous path. That's what the devil comes to do because he comes around only to steal, kill and destroy. But Jesus came to give us life — abundant life (John 10:10).

Abundance in every area, a full life, a good plan, unstoppable increase... That is God's best for you.

Friend, there is a future for you! There's a new season of abundance coming to God's people. But it's coming only into the lives of people who are willing to do what the Lord has instructed us to do. There's a new season coming — He wants *you* to have a new season of abundance, blessing and increase. But it's only coming to those who obey Him.

Yes, that includes sowing your seed. But it also includes having the right attitude, listening to His Word and hiding it in your heart, and acting on your faith in Him. The God kind of increase is about so much more than money. The biblical principle of what my Dad, Oral Roberts, called *seed faith* is about every area of your life, because God cares about every part of you — spirit, soul, and body.

This is something I learned at my father's knee. In fact, I often tell people that Oral Roberts was not just my father in the physical sense, but he was also my father in a spiritual sense—he was my *spiritual mentor.*

My dad talked to me many times about the importance of increase (seed faith) in my life because He wanted to be sure I got it down in my spirit. And now I want to do the same thing for you...because I know that getting into obedience and agreement with God's path to unstoppable increase is as important to your life as breathing out and breathing in. One function needs to follow the other in order for everything to work like God intended.

I'm so excited to share with you these powerful biblical principles to help you be free from bondage to debt, free from lack and need, fulfilled in your job, overflowing in your finances, and able to be a blessing to the world by sharing the abundance you have with those in need, in Jesus' name.

So, as you read, please read this book in faith, expecting God to open your eyes to what you can do to put yourself in position to receive all He has for you! Get ready to step into a future of unstoppable increase!

Important Points to Remember

1. God is bringing new seasons of blessing and increase into the lives of those who sow in faith.
2. Those who commit to doing things God's way will see more and more increase in their lives. Those who don't sow will not experience these seasons of blessing and increase.
3. God's blessings don't come automatically. We must first get into position to receive them.
4. In partnership with God, we can accomplish amazing things.
5. Increase from God comes in the form of blessings in every area of life. The principle of seed-faith applies to every area of life, not just finances.

Prayer Points

1. Lord, help me to know and recognize Your kind of increase every time it shows up in my life.
2. Lord, help me to receive the blessings You send my way. Help me to position myself to receive. Open my eyes to all the ways I can do so.

Scriptures for Further Study

Revelation 3:8
Deuteronomy 28:1–13
Jeremiah 29:11
John 10:10

Chapter 2

Increase Begins with a Seed

Nevertheless, at Your word I will let down the net.

— Luke 5:5

The first part of any harvest — spiritual, natural, physical, financial, relational or any other harvest — is the sowing of a seed. God promises that seed time and harvest will not fail. The Bible tells us, *While the earth remains, seedtime and harvest, cold and heat, winter and summer, and day and night shall not cease* (Genesis 8:22). So, if we want to experience abundant increase in our lives, we need to start with a seed.

Let me give you an example from the Bible where you can see how our seeds — the things we do and give to the Lord in faith — lead us to receive blessings from Him.

Sharing a Boat Becomes a Seed

In Luke chapter five, I want you to meet a man by the name of Peter. Peter was sitting on the shores of the Sea of Galilee. Now it was daytime, and Peter was a fisherman.

So, he was washing and mending his nets when Jesus came walking up and said to him, "Lend me your boat."

Can you picture something like that happening to you? What would you say? I imagine Peter probably said something like, "What do you want my boat for?"

I imagine Jesus probably responded, "I want to preach from it. There's a large crowd here. If you loan me your boat and push me out a little bit in the water, the water will help magnify my voice, and I can preach to this great crowd."

We can't know exactly what Peter was thinking at that moment, but we know the result: he lent Jesus his boat.

Jesus preached to the crowd. No doubt, Peter must have heard the message as he stood there, waiting to get his boat back. And while Luke doesn't tell us what the message was, we know it must have been full of power and anointing, full of the Holy Ghost and healing, because that's who Jesus was and it's what He preached throughout His ministry.

In other words, Peter heard a word that challenged his faith.

When Jesus finished ministering, He came back to Peter and said, "Now, launch out into the deep waters, and let down your nets for a catch." I want you to notice a few things about what Jesus said.

First of all, He used the plural word, *nets*. "Let down your *nets* for a catch." He was anticipating that the catch would be so big — the increase to Peter's situation so significant — that it would take more than one net to contain all the fish.

But Peter didn't seem to understand or believe what Jesus was saying. He responded, "Master, we fished all night last night, and we didn't catch a thing." In other words, Peter was *not* expecting a big catch of anything, and here's why.

In those days, fishermen did their job in the dark, during the night, because the waters of the Sea of Galilee are crystal clear. If you throw a net into the water, the fish can see it and swim the other way. So Peter and his crew fished at night, when the fish couldn't see and avoid the net.

Peter had fished the night before, as was his usual custom as a well-trained fisherman, but he and his crew had caught nothing. They landed no fish during the night when it was easiest to bring in a catch. So, you can imagine his doubts when Jesus suggested fishing during the daylight, when a good catch was even more unlikely to happen.

Next, Jesus had the audacity to say to Peter, "Launch out into the deep waters." He was expecting that catch to happen away from the shore.

But that, too, must have sounded hard to believe to Peter's ears. You see, the Sea of Galilee is 200 feet below sea level, and it's subject to violent storms almost without notice. In the flash of a second, a storm could rise up. And these storms were often deadly. If a small fishing boat sailed out to the middle of the sea, a sudden storm could turn the boat over with ease.

In those days, the little fishing boats Peter and his men used would not have been strong enough to withstand the Sea of Galiee's dangerous power in bad weather. Those fishing boats would have been destroyed. Everyone on the boat would have likely perished. So, he and all the other fishermen of his day fished along the shore, where it was much safer.

Here's the thing, though. When you fish along the shore, you catch small fish. You don't catch big fish, because the big fish are out in the deep waters where they have room to swim and grow. It's safer to fish by the shore, but it's not likely to bring you a significant increase in the number or size of the fish you catch.

So when Peter said, "Master, we fished all night last night, and we didn't catch a thing," I believe he was really saying, "Jesus, we've kept all the rules. We fished at night, but we got nothing. We fished along the shoreline as we always do, but we took no fish, not even any little ones like we usually do. I know You probably mean well, but Your idea just won't work."

Your Seed Must Be Linked to Your Faith

We've all been there, right? We've heard from the Lord, yet what He has told us to do seems impossible to believe or expect. I'm sure you can relate. If you've spent any time at all serving the Lord, you have surely experienced what Peter was experiencing right at that moment.

Why? Because any sort of miracle involves using faith. And faith is needed at times when we can't do it on our own.

I believe that's what Jesus was getting at when He told Peter, "Launch out into the deep waters, and let down your nets for a catch." He wasn't ignorant of how fishing worked on the Sea of Galilee. He was focused on how God works in our lives, which is something Peter wasn't familiar with.

I believe Jesus was saying, "Launch out into the deep, because that's where the miracles are. That's where your faith can come to life! You heard My message, Peter. Now, let Me bring a miracle into your life."

That word *now* is an important word. The God we serve is a "right now God." He's not a yesterday God. He's not an earlier this morning God. He's not a last night we didn't catch any fish God. He's a right now God. If you want to experience a miracle, you can't stay focused on and fixed in the past. You have to reach out in faith to Him *now* for miracles *now.*

Jesus said, "Now, Peter, now, launch out into the deep waters for a catch. You've been fishing along the shoreline, but you need some big miracles. The big miracles are out there, Peter. They're not here by the shore. They're out there in the deep where you have to use your faith as a seed! Launch out into the deep. Let down your nets for a catch."

And Peter said, "Well, okay. Because you say so, I'll do it."

I don't know exactly what Peter was thinking at that moment. He probably had some doubts and some questions. But the most important thing that Peter did was that he made a decision to trust God in spite of his questions and any doubts.

When God speaks to you and tells you to do something, I promise you it will go against your mind. Your mind will say, "No, no, no, that's not right. That goes against everything that I know." But I have news for you. God knows better than you. His ways are above your ways. His thoughts are above your thoughts (Isaiah 55:8–9). And He takes the things that the world calls foolish and uses them to confound the wise (1 Corinthians 1:27).

It's a good thing for us to say, "Jesus, because You say so, I'll obey You. I may not understand it. I may not know how it's all going to work out, but because You said so, Jesus, I'll do it." I believe that's how a miracle starts. That's how our increase comes — as we step out in faith to do what Jesus tells us to do, trusting Him to do what is needed to bring the miracle about.

Faith Brings Miracles into Your Boat

After Peter agreed to do what Jesus said, he acted on it. He got into his boat and headed out into the deep waters where the big fish were. And when he threw the net over, suddenly his shoulders tightened as he felt something hit the net. He began to haul the net in. And what he saw shocked him.

That single net was filled with an enormous catch of fish — in broad daylight, away from the shore, where catches like that just didn't happen. It was a miracle in the making!

As Peter and his men hauled in the net, it began to break. Remember, Peter had said, "I'll throw out *a* net." Jesus wanted to give him an even bigger miracle. He had said, "Let down your *nets*." Peter only put one net into the water. If he had used more than one, he could have gotten an even bigger miracle.

I often wonder why that net began to break. Maybe it wasn't Peter's best net. You know, when you obey God, you need to go all the way. You need to give Him your best. Peter gave Him one net, and maybe it wasn't even the best net he had. When he hauled it in, it broke. And fish were swimming through the holes and escaping — big fish, worth $5, $10, $20, maybe even $100 each.

There were so many fish that Peter called on his partners in another boat to come help him. So, they came over. And while Peter was hauling in his net with the fish falling out because it was broken, his partners came over and put down their nets, and their nets were filled. Peter's net was filled. And the boat began to sink. It was a net-breaking, boat-sinking load of miracles.

In that moment, as Peter saw the catch he had...and the even bigger catch he could have had if he'd given God more to work with... he recognized that he had shortchanged God. He had only gone part way in his obedience. The Bible says he got down on his knees and said these words to Jesus: "Lord, depart from me. I've missed it, Jesus. I didn't even do completely what You said. Depart from me, because I'm a sinful man."

But Jesus said, "No, Peter, no. You get up and do things differently from now on. And I'll make you a fisher of men. I'll make something out of your life."

Through that experience Peter had of planting the seed of his boat, he got a net-breaking, boat-sinking load of miracle fish. And it wasn't long until he quit his fishing business and went full time into ministry with Jesus.

Something extraordinary must have happened to Peter in those next three years because the next time we see him fishing, he wasn't using a net. He wasn't even using bait on his hook! The next time he went fishing, he did something unusual, because during those three years he had been schooled in faith.

His faith was so strong that he could act on it immediately when Jesus said, "Throw in a hook. And the first fish you catch will have money in its mouth." Sure enough, Peter did it and the fish had money in its mouth, enough to pay the taxes he and Jesus owed (Matthew 17:27).

During those three and a half years, Peter had some amazing displays of faith! When Jesus asked the question, "Who do you say I am?" it was Peter who replied, "You are the Christ, the son of the living God." And Jesus replied, "Flesh and blood hasn't revealed this to you, Peter, but My father in heaven has revealed this to you. And upon this rock of revelation, Peter, because you know who I am, I'll build My church. And the gates of hell shall not prevail against it."

Even though he fell short and denied Jesus three and a half years later during his trial and crucifixion, Peter later repented and turned into a powerful preacher! Even though Peter experienced a shortcoming, like many of us have, it was Peter on the day of Pentecost who preached a message that led 3,000 people to give their lives to Christ. And the church was born that day (Acts 2:14–41).

It was Peter who was so anointed and full of God that when he came to town, people would lay their sick on cots or mats in the street so Peter's shadow might cover them, and they were healed (Acts 5:15).

Peter learned a tremendous principle that day on the Sea of Galilee with Jesus. When you sow unto God, God opens the windows of heaven and pours out a blessing so great that there's not room enough to receive it (Malachi 3:10–11).

God sets the rules, but we have to jump in and do what He says. He isn't going to plant your seed for you. That's our job. But as you sow to God, He's the one who is responsible for bringing about the harvest. Sowing the seed is our job, and bringing the increase is His job. He is the One who opens the windows of heaven to pour out a blessing where there's not room enough to receive it.

Sowing and reaping, giving and receiving, is a biblical principle. It's a godly system. It's a true system, and it works. But you and I must do our part. And when we do, then God does His part, and we see miracles!

Important Points to Remember

1. The first part of any harvest is the sowing of a seed.
2. When Jesus borrowed Peter's boat, it was after delivering a message to the crowd that challenged Peter's faith.
3. Any miracle you receive involves using faith to receive it.
4. If you need a miracle now, the time to reach out in faith to Him is now. Don't dwell on past failures or losses. Focus on what God can do for you right now.
5. Our acts of faith now prepare us for bigger acts of faith and harvests later on.
6. God sets the rules, but we must act on them to receive results. When we do our part, He does His part.

Prayer Points

1. Lord, give me seeds to sow and give me wisdom when and where to sow them so that I am sowing in line with Your will.
2. Strengthen me, Lord, to act in faith and to expect miracles.
3. Like the apostle Peter, may I grow ever stronger in faith as I live for You.

Scriptures for Further Study

Luke 5:5
Genesis 8:22
Luke 5:1–11
Isaiah 55:8–9
1 Corinthians 1:27
Matthew 17:27
Acts 2:14–41
Acts 5:15
Malachi 3:10–11

Chapter 3

IS MONEY GOOD OR BAD?

For the love of money is a root of all kinds of evil, for which some have strayed from the faith in their greediness, and pierced themselves through with many sorrows.

— 1 Timothy 6:10

Now, there's a lot of talk about giving today. And even Christians aren't always sure what God's Word says about money and abundance and prosperity. In this chapter, I want to address the question in many minds — is having money good, or is it evil? How does God feel about money?

Is It Godly to Prosper?

You know, the world doesn't seem to have a problem with prospering. It's easy to turn on the news and see stories about people who are prospering in big businesses or celebrities who are earning fortune and fame. We may see some of their excesses or their failures to use their wealth wisely and think that it is bad to be wealthy.

There are even some Christians who have a problem with prosperity. My dad used to say that when he was a young preacher, the people had the attitude, "If God will keep Oral Roberts humble, we will keep him poor."

Well, that's a terrible thing. It's terrible to be poor, and it is terrible to expect those who serve God to live in poverty. That's a lie that Satan has tried to put on people over the years. There is no scriptural basis to it, no Bible verse that says God expects Christians to be poor.

In fact, it's very much the opposite! It is God's plan for the righteous to prosper and have more than enough to meet their needs. And who are the righteous? That's *you*! As long as you're a born-again, blood-bought believer in Jesus Christ as your Lord and Savior, then according to the scriptures, you are counted as righteous in Christ according to 2 Corinthians 5:21, and God has a plan to help you live abundantly.

You may say, "Richard, how can you be so sure that God wants me to prosper?" The answer is found in God's own Word! He said in 3 John 2, *Beloved, I pray that you may prosper in all things and be in health, just as your soul prospers.*

I want you to know beyond any shadow of a doubt that it's God's will for you to prosper. He wants you to prosper in your mind, your family, your job, your finances, your health — in every area of your life from the crown of your head to the soles of your feet.

A Common Misconception about Wealth

If God's Word says that His children are meant to have more than enough to meet their needs and sow into the work of His kingdom, then where does the idea that God wants His people to be poor come from? I believe it comes from a misquoted scripture that people have not fully understood.

You'll hear it when people quote a common saying: "Money is the root of all evil." You've probably heard someone say it before.

But that's not what the Bible says. The Bible doesn't say *money* is the root of all evil. If it was, then Jesus died for the wrong reason — He should have conquered money instead of sin! But no, Jesus died for sin, which is the ultimate cause of the evil in the world.

So, what does God's Word *actually* say about money? First Timothy 6:10 says, *For the LOVE of money is a root of all kinds of evil, for which some have strayed from the faith in their greediness, and pierced themselves through with many sorrows.*

I want you to know that there's nothing wrong with money, in and of itself. You have to have money to pay your bills, buy groceries, and keep a roof over your head. Money is the acceptable medium of exchange for goods and services.

My dad taught me that money is like a walking stick. Money exists to help you get where you need to go. Money is neither good nor bad. It takes after the person who's using it.

That's why in Titus 1:11 (KJV) Paul called it "filthy luchre." It wasn't because the money itself was evil. But the people using that money were using it in a filthy, evil, harmful way. The people Paul was speaking of in Titus chapter 1 were teaching wrong things and leading people astray and disrupting households. They were doing wrong. They were pursuing *dishonest gain*.

But Paul doesn't always call money "filthy." In Philippians chapter 4, he is speaking to a group of Christians who were giving offerings to help him preach the Gospel and do the work of God. Paul said the Philippians' gifts were *a sweet-smelling aroma, an acceptable sacrifice, well pleasing to God* (v. 18). He referred to that money as *sweet-smelling* because of the way that the Philippian Christians were using it.

It's not the money itself that is good or evil. The issue is the *choice* we make. It is how we *choose* to use money that produces good or evil.

How We Handle Our Money Matters to God

I've already said that many Christians believe it is wrong to have money. But there are some who err on the other side, believing that simply because they are Christians, they are bound to prosper exceedingly.

I believe that's the result of a misunderstanding about another scripture, Proverbs 13:22, which says, *A good man leaves an inheritance to his children's children, but the wealth of the sinner is stored up for the righteous.* Many read that and say, "Oh, I'm going to get the wealth of the wicked because it is laid up for the righteous," and then they don't do anything to receive it.

But that's a mistake. You see, a Christian doesn't automatically receive the wealth of the wicked, any more than a sinner is going to get to heaven just because Jesus died for him, or a sick person is going to be healed simply because Jesus is a Healer.

If you want to be saved, you must follow God's rules of receiving salvation by believing in Jesus and confessing that He is your Lord and Savior. If you want to be healed, you must release your faith and do what God's Word says concerning healing. And if you want to enjoy God's abundant living, you must do what He says to do in His Word concerning your finances, your giving, your tithes and your offerings.

Even in Malachi 3:7 when God speaks of why Israel was failing to prosper, He said, "*You have gone away from My ordinances.*" They were not obeying the Lord or using their money according to His will and His Word.

The Most Important Part of Prosperity

The most important thing in life is not money. It's that you love God with your heart, soul, mind and strength (Matthew 22:37)...and that you keep His commandments and do what His Word says (John 14:15)... and that you joyfully sow your seed to Him in faith (2 Corinthians 9:7). Our love... our faith...our obedience to God...that's what matters most to God, because it's our relationship with Him that helps us make good choices about how we earn and spend our finances.

Once God is truly at the center of our lives, I believe we can begin to expect God's abundance. I believe that God wants His people to prosper in every area of life, just as He says in 3 John 2. He wants us to have unstoppable increase! But the only way to receive His increase is to do what the Word of God says.

No matter what is going on in the world around us, we can choose to remain focused on the Word of God, and we can get our needs met. And we can believe that He will open to us the windows of heaven as we make Him the Lord of our lives. As we give unto Him the way the Bible tells us to do, we can watch Him open those windows of heaven and pour us out a blessing in the way that we need it most.

I believe this is God's will for you. He is the One *who has given you the power to get wealth* (Deuteronomy 8:18). Let that get into your spirit. God wants you to have unstoppable increase, and it starts by making Him first in your life, and keeping His Word, and then planting your seed unto Him and expecting Him to bless it back to you — *good measure, pressed down, shaken together and running over* (Luke 6:38).

Important Points to Remember

1. There is no scriptural basis to the belief that to be godly, you must also be poor.
2. In fact, God's plan according to 3 John 2 is for the righteous to prosper and have more than enough to meet their needs and reach out to others for Christ's sake.
3. Money is a means of exchange and is not evil in and of itself. It is how we use money, and our attitudes toward money, that can be good or evil.
4. As we focus on and come into alignment with God's ways of doing and being, we become better equipped to use money wisely and in a godly way.

Prayer Points

1. Help me, Lord, to live my life according to Your ways. Teach me to do Your will in all things, including how I view money and how I use money.
2. If I have any attitudes toward money that are not right in Your eyes, reveal the truth to me and help me to see finances and prosperity as You see them.
3. Help me to always remember that You give me the ability to grow and increase financially, and help me to honor You in all I do with the fruits of that increase.

Scriptures for Further Study

1 Timothy 6:10
3 John 2
Titus 1:11
Philippians 4:18
Proverbs 13:22

Malachi 3:7
Matthew 22:37
John 14:15
2 Corinthians 9:7
Deuteronomy 8:18
Luke 6:38

Chapter 4

Can You Buy a Miracle?

For us there is one God, the Father, of whom are all things, and we for Him; and one Lord Jesus Christ, through whom are all things, and through whom we live.

— 1 Corinthians 8:6

Often on my television program or during the healing services I conduct throughout the year, I encourage people to plant a seed of their faith and expect God to use it for His glory, then multiply it back in the way they need it most.

If you've heard me say this over the years, and if you've followed this ministry, you probably already know about sowing seeds in faith. But many people don't know about this biblical concept. I have had people hear me talk about sowing a seed and then say to me, "Richard, do you mean I can give you money, and I can buy my healing?"

No, I certainly don't mean that. You can't buy healing. You can't buy any kind of miracle from God. That's not what seed faith is about.

Money Can't Buy a Miracle

Simply put, healing is not for sale. Miracles aren't for sale. God doesn't work that way. If you could buy a miracle from God, I think most people would go to the bank and empty out their accounts in order to get one. And we'd be hearing story after story about how those who could afford it were buying the miracles they need.

But that's not happening, because God doesn't work that way. For one thing, the Bible tells us clearly that God does not show favoritism (Acts 10:34; Romans 2:11). If money could buy miracles, then those with money would have all of God's many blessings, while those without it would not receive anything from God because they couldn't afford it. Now, that's showing favoritism, isn't it? And the Bible says God doesn't do that.

And who would decide the value placed on each person's need? For instance, what would be the "going rate" for a healing from cancer, or a heart condition, or a broken leg, or any other physical problem? That would be impossible to determine, wouldn't it?

And that's just the physical aspect of healing. Think of someone with a broken heart, or a broken marriage, or a child who has gone missing and no one knows where they are. There is no price you could set on any of those things.

No, there is no way to "buy" a miracle because our needs

can't be quantified in financial terms. God does not need our money. Money is not the source of miracles.

So, where do miracles come from? The Apostle Paul tells us, *For us there is one God, the Father, OF WHOM ARE ALL THINGS, and we for Him; and one Lord Jesus Christ, THROUGH WHOM ARE ALL THINGS, and through whom we live* (1 Corinthians 8:6). God is the source of miracles. He is the source of all things.

That's why I always say that God is my source. Philippians 4:19 says, *My God shall supply all your need according to His riches in glory by Christ Jesus.* God will supply all our needs according to His riches, His love for us, His power to help us, and His wisdom to guide us. He may use many different means to get us what we need — a job, gifts, doctors, friends, family and other methods — to meet our need.

But God alone is the source, and He alone cannot fail.

Why Plant a Seed?

So if money can't buy miracles, why do I encourage people to plant seeds of their faith toward God?

Well, first of all, I believe that when you plant a seed of your faith to the Lord — when you give Him something that is of real value to you and requires your heart to be involved in the giving — you put yourself in position for receiving a miracle. We see this principle in Malachi 3:10–11 where God said, "*Bring all the tithes into the storehouse, that there may be food* (resources) *in My house, and try Me now in this," says the Lord of hosts, "if I will not open for you the windows of heaven and pour out for you such blessing that there will not be room enough to receive it. And I will rebuke the devourer for your sakes...*"

The Bible doesn't say you can buy your miracle. It says that when you sow your seed, you have a right to ask God to rebuke the devourer — the devil — for your sake. Why? Because when you sow a seed, the Bible says you are to receive a harvest because harvests always follow seed-sowing (Genesis 8:22).

What Is a Seed of Our Faith?

Once we understand that God is our source, we must do something to tap into what He has for us. We must connect to the source so we can receive from Him. How do we do that? Jesus told us how.

First of all, He said, *If you can believe, all things are possible to him who believes* (Mark 9:23). We receive God's promises, His blessings, by believing Him. In other words, we receive from Him through faith. That's why I call what you are giving to God a seed of *faith*. It is our faith that we are giving to God.

Second, we are to *give first*, and then expect our harvest to follow. Luke 6:38 says, *Give, and it shall be given unto you.* We must first plant a seed of faith so that God can multiply it back to meet our need. It takes faith to give first and then expect a harvest. But this is the way God has ordained for us to receive from Him.

Notice again that Luke 6:38 says, *Give.* I believe Jesus is talking about giving in the deepest sense of the word — the giving of ourselves to God. This includes anything we can give — love, time, patience, forgiveness, finances, prayer, whatever we have. Your seeds can be anything you have to offer, anything appropriate to the situation.

If you want friends, you can sow love and compassion and time to other people, trusting God for a harvest of godly friends in your life. If you need a healing, you sow the seed of your prayers for others who are ill, and expect God to heal both them and you in a harvest of well-being. Anything can be a seed sown to God — as long as it is sown in faith, with you believing and expecting to see a harvest from the Lord.

You see, our giving reflects our trust in God and our thankfulness. It links us to God's inexhaustible resources for our every need. There is no way we can give to God without receiving something back from Him, multiplied! When you plant your seed, you have a Bible right to expect God to use it for His glory and then multiply it back to you in the form of a harvest to meet your needs (Luke 6:38).

Expect Your Harvest

The moment we ask God for something — the moment we do our part and plant our seed of faith — we should believe God that the answer is on its way. It is important to expect our miracle so we can recognize it and reach forth to take it when it comes.

And it's also important to remember that God controls the time and method He will use to give back to us. We must keep trusting God and expecting our miracle, no matter how long it takes to reach us. He is faithful to hear us and respond to us (1 John 5:14–15). We don't need to fear that He won't take care of us. Instead, we are to stay in faith, expecting a harvest from our seeds of faith, until the harvest arrives.

So, give God something to work with. No matter how little you think you have, sow it in joy and faith, knowing in your heart that you are sowing seed so you may reap miracles. Then start expecting all kinds of miracles! Remember, God always sends the right answer at the right time, in the right way. His timing and methods are always exactly right for our lives!

Important Points to Remember

1. Miracles are not for sale. God doesn't work that way. It is impossible to buy a miracle from God because God does not need our money.
2. What God responds to is our faith in Him. As we act on our faith in His Word, it is productive for opening our lives to His miracle-working power.
3. For many people, sowing a seed in faith is a way to release their faith in God. In this sense, sowing a seed is useful as you believe God to meet your specific, personal needs.
4. Anything you give in faith, believing that God has answers for you, can be a seed — including love, time, patience, forgiveness, prayer and finances.
5. Whenever you give anything in faith, start believing and expecting that God has heard your prayers and is sending you a harvest (1 John 5:14–15, Luke 6:38).

Prayer Points

1. Lord, forgive me and set me free from any confusion, doubt or frustration I have had about sowing seeds, giving in faith, or receiving miracles that have been revealed to me as I have read this chapter.
2. Show me where I can begin to sow seeds of what I have. Show me ways to give the love, time, patience, forgiveness, prayer, finances and other resources I have available.
3. I trust You to provide me with harvests, to hear my prayers, and to meet my needs as I give and act according to Your Word and my faith in You.

Scriptures for Further Study

1 Corinthians 8:6
Acts 10:34
Romans 2:11
1 Corinthians 8:6
Philippians 4:19
Malachi 3:10–11
Genesis 8:22
Mark 9:23
Luke 6:38
1 John 5:14–15

Chapter 5

DEVELOPING THE RIGHT ATTITUDE FOR INCREASE

I am full, having received from Epaphroditus the things sent from you, a sweet-smelling aroma, an acceptable sacrifice, well pleasing to God. And my God shall supply all your need according to His riches in glory by Christ Jesus.

— Philippians 4:18–19

One of the Scriptures my Dad poured into me as I grew up was Philippians 4:13–19, which reads as follows:

I can do all things through Christ who strengthens me. Nevertheless you have done well that you shared in my distress. Now you Philippians know also that in the beginning of the gospel, when I departed from Macedonia, no church shared with me concerning giving and receiving but you only. For even in Thessalonica you sent aid once and again for my necessities. Not that I seek the gift, but I seek the fruit that abounds to your account. Indeed I have all and abound. I am full, having received from Epaphroditus the things sent from you, a sweet-smelling aroma, an acceptable sacrifice, well pleasing to God. And my God shall supply all your need according to His riches in glory by Christ Jesus.

These verses of scripture give us powerful insights into how God desires for us to view giving and receiving. They reveal how you can develop the right attitude to sow seeds and reap the harvests of increase that the Lord has for you.

The Key to Giving that the Philippian Church Understood

Paul had established this Philippian church. He had, no doubt, shared his testimony with them of how he was knocked down and blinded on his way to Damascus to persecute and kill Christians…how he'd heard a voice — the voice of Jesus — asking, "Saul, Saul" (his Jewish name), "why do you persecute Me?"

And he most likely told them how he was led to a certain house to a man named Ananias who prayed for him. As Ananias laid his hands on him, the scales fell from Paul's eyes, spiritually as well as physically, and he had a true encounter with God (Acts 9:1–22).

So the Philippians knew Paul's story, what he had already suffered for the Lord, and how he had zeal and passion to share the Gospel. But the Philippians also came to understand something very important — a key to increase — that sets them apart from the other churches in the New Testament.

You see, many other churches were also established by Paul during his ministry, and surely they all knew his story. In that way, those other churches were no different than the Philippians. Yet the Philippians were the only Christians that Paul commended so powerfully for their giving, and they are the ones who received a special promise from the Lord that *He shall supply all your need according to His riches in glory by Christ Jesus* (Philippians 4:19).

So, what was the key to giving that the Christians in Philippi understood?

I believe the Philippians understood that the greater the sacrifice, the greater the blessing. Paul poured into them what God had poured into him, just as he did with the other churches he started. But these Philippians were the only group who did something about it. They gave *once and again* to Paul's need—which had to do with spreading the Gospel. That means they didn't just give once. I believe they got into a lifestyle of giving. And they understood receiving as well.

The Philippians had the right motive in giving, and Paul had the right motive in asking. "*Not that I desire a gift*," Paul said, "*but I desire fruit that may abound to your account*" (v. 17). In other words, he wasn't trying to get something *from* them; he was trying to get something *to* them. And, apparently, he was successful at that because the Philippians didn't just give. They also received God's promise of a harvest of increase!

Giving Is Part of Our Covenant with God

In a way, Paul taught the Philippians how to put God to the test and prove His faithfulness. He taught them how to see for themselves what God would do on their behalf if they kept on giving with the right attitude. Let me explain what I mean.

My dad often spoke about what he called our "blessing-pact covenant with God." Once when I asked him what he meant by that term, he explained it like this.

He said, "Richard, the Apostle Paul taught it and the Philippians understood it — the principles that the Book of Malachi laid out. When you bring your giving unto the Lord, He opens the windows of heaven and pours you out a blessing where there isn't even room enough to receive it. But He doesn't just stop there; He also rebukes the devourer — the devil — for our sakes (Malachi 3:10–11). That's the blessing-pact covenant with God."

Once when my dad was preaching on the road, he got thirsty in his hotel room. With a couple of quarters in his hand, he went down the hallway and found a soft drink machine. After he put his money in and made his selection, he said that he just automatically reached down with the same hand to receive his selection.

He said, "Richard, when I did that, it hit me that there was a contract between the maker of that product and the owner of the machine that sold it. And when I, as a third party, entered into that contract, I had a right to expect that contract to be made good and provide me with my soft drink selection."

Then Dad said, "If we can enter into a contract with a company that makes a soft drink machine, how much more can we enter into a covenant, or a contract, with God who made everything?"

That's the blessing-pact covenant we have with God. When we bring our offerings to Him and fulfill our part of the biblical contract, He opens the windows of heaven and fulfills His part of the contract.

We can be just like the Philippians, no matter what the economy may look like. When others are saying, "No, I've got to hold on to what I have," we can say, "Now is the time that I must sow to the Lord." We can do it by faith! And we can expect to receive everything we need from God, because like the Philippians, we know God, we can operate by faith in giving and receiving, and our giving will prove God's faithfulness.

Give in Faith, Not Fear

Another key to maintaining the right attitude toward giving is that you don't want to give — or fail to give — in an attitude of fear. *For God has not given us a spirit of fear, but of power and of love and of a sound mind* (2 Timothy 1:7). We have the promises of God on our side! When we act in faith on His promises, we can expect Him to bring them to pass on our behalf.

This is not the time to live in fear, but in power — the power of seed faith. This is not the time to hold back, but *to sow*... to *prove* God to be the God of blessing that He says He is, and to *put ourselves in position* to receive those blessings from His hand.

Paul said that the Philippian church's giving was an acceptable sacrifice in God's eyes. He said it was sweet smelling. When you use your money for God's kingdom and you give it in faith, expecting a harvest, then your giving is an acceptable, sweet sacrifice, well-pleasing to God.

Hebrews 11:6 says, *Without faith, it is impossible to please Him.* Don't miss this. You can't please God unless you are acting in faith. So, if the Philippians' gift was pleasing to Him, then it means their gift had their faith attached to it.

Give God Your Best

A third key to having the right attitude toward giving is that when you sow, you are to give God your best. Then ask Him for His best. Remember, the greater the sacrifice, the greater the blessing.

God does not want you to give something indiscriminately. He does not want you to give in such a way that it means nothing to you. If it means nothing to you, it won't mean anything to Him either.

Some people approach their giving with an attitude that says, "Well, I have something over here that I won't miss. So therefore, I will give it to God." I've seen it happen as people donate to their church or to missions or other ministries. They may say, "I've worn this dress, this shirt, these pants, for ten years now. They're frayed. They're old. All the color has faded out of them. I believe I'll just donate them to somebody, and this will be my seed faith gift."

Can you imagine being on the receiving end of that gift? If someone said to you, "This is my old junk; you can have it," what would you think? Would it feel generous to you? I doubt it! I believe that your giving must cost you something.

There must be something of value in your gift; it must mean something to you.

There's a story in 1 Chronicles 21, and it illustrates the biblical principle that you must give something of value. Here's what happened:

At the time, David was king of Israel. And David made a horrible mistake which cost a lot of lives. He decided, against the will of God, that He would number the men of Israel. His leading general tried to talk him out of it, but David would not hear of it. He went ahead and disobeyed God and numbered the people.

Why did God not want him to number the people? I don't know; the Bible doesn't say. But the Bible does say that God was very displeased with David for doing it. The Lord sent a prophet named Gad to David to tell him that he had displeased the Lord. As soon as David heard that message, he immediately began to repent.

Gad said, "The Lord sent me to tell you that because of what you've done, there are three things that could happen to you, and you can have your choice. You can either have famine for three years, or you can have your enemies overrunning you for three months, or you can have three days of plague. Which one would you like?"

Well, I'm sure David didn't want any of them. But he had to choose. So he said, "Let us fall in the hands of the Lord." For three days, a plague was set loose in the land, and 70,000 men lost their lives. After those terrible three days, the Lord spoke to David and told him to offer a sacrifice, and to buy the threshing floor where a man named Araunah the Jebusite was working.

David approached Araunah and said, "I want to buy this threshing floor."

Araunah said, "No, King David. You don't have to buy it. I will give it to you."

David responded in an interesting, powerful way. He said, "No, you won't give it to me. I will buy it. And I will pay the full price, no discount."

Well, why the full price? Because David had done something wrong in the sight of God. People lost their lives because of David's sin, and he wanted and needed to do what the Lord said to make things right again. Thus, he said, "I would not give God that which costs me nothing."

Your gift to God must mean something to you. If it doesn't mean anything to you, I promise you it won't mean anything to God. You can't say, "I won't miss this, so I'll just give it to somebody." That's what I call indiscriminate giving. I don't believe that God will bless that.

David knew that. He knew that his sacrifice, his gift to God, had to mean something because the lives of Israelites hung in the balance. So David bought the threshing floor at the full price, as well as the animals and the tools, and he made his sacrifice to the Lord. And God accepted the offering, and the plague stopped.

If you study the Bible, you'll find that Araunah's threshing floor is the place where David's son Solomon built the temple of the Lord. It's on Mount Moriah. The temple of Israel was built on that very spot where David said, "I would not give God that which costs me nothing."

In this world, many people want something for nothing. God is saying, "Don't treat Me that way. When you give to Me, give Me something that means something to you."

If God speaks to you and tells you to give an article of clothing to someone, don't go to your closet and grab the oldest thing you can find. Give God your best. Give something new that's in your closet, or go to the store and buy something nice to give away.

Remember what Matthew 7:2 says: *With the same measure you use, it will be measured back to you.* The way you bless others is the same way God may bless you someday. Don't try to get something for nothing.

Give Sincerely and from Your Heart

Finally, when you give, give with an honest, sincere heart. Luke 6:45 says, *A good man out of the good treasure of his heart brings forth good; and an evil man out of the evil treasure of his heart brings forth evil.* Whatever is in your heart will eventually come out. It is just like what happens when you squeeze a lemon; whatever is on the inside will come out. So it's important to make sure that you are giving out of a heart that is good, with motives that are pure and holy. When you give that way, according to Luke 6:45, that's how you'll receive. Your right-hearted giving brings forth good, not evil.

If you are not a regular giver, I encourage you to search your heart and make a change. Ask the Lord to help you to be generous and committed in your giving, and trust Him to take care of you. He will do it if you'll let Him, so you don't have to let fear rule your heart. Let faith rule your heart instead, and I believe you'll begin to see His many blessings of increase in your life.

Important Points to Remember

1. The church at Philippi stands out in the New Testament as a group of believers who understood the value and importance of regularly giving to the work of God that the apostle Paul was doing. For this reason, they not only gave but they received from the Lord as well.
2. It is important to see our giving as part of our covenant with God, and trust in Him that as we do our part by giving in faith, He will do His part by sending us harvests of His blessings.
3. We are to give to God and sow our seeds in faith, not in fear.
4. When we give, we are to give God our best, and then ask Him for and expect His best.
5. Finally, when we give, we are to give sincerely and from our heart, with motives that are pure and holy.

Prayer Points

1. Search me, oh God, and know my heart. Show me if there is any attitude or belief within me concerning giving that is not of You.
2. Help me to grow in faith for both giving and receiving.
3. Deliver me from any and all fears concerning giving, receiving, finances and money.
4. May my motives in giving and receiving always be pure and holy in Your sight.

Scriptures for Further Study

Philippians 4:13–19
Acts 9:1–22
Malachi 3:10–11

2 Timothy 1:7
Hebrews 11:6
1 Chronicles 21:21–26
Matthew 7:2
Luke 6:45

Chapter 6

We Give When We Know Who God Is

I will make you a great nation; I will bless you and make your name great; and you shall be a blessing.

— Genesis 12:2

When we think of the God kind of increase, one man comes to mind right away — a man who enjoyed as much abundance as anyone who has ever lived. His name was Abraham.

Now, Abraham was born in a place called Ur of the Chaldees, or what you and I know today as Iraq. He and his wife, Sarah, were living among pagans at the time, and they didn't know anything about God until one day, as the Bible tells us, they heard the voice of the Lord.

The Lord said, *Get out of your country, from your family and from your father's house, to a land that I will show you. I will make you a great nation; I will bless you and make your name great; and you shall be a blessing. I will bless those who bless you, and I will curse him who curses you; and in you all the families of the earth shall be blessed* (Genesis 12:1–3).

Imagine God speaking to you and saying, "Get in your car and start driving. I'll tell you where you're going when you get there." That's basically what happened to Abraham. What's interesting is that he and his wife obeyed. That's the first step to following God straight into unstoppable increase — obeying Him.

The Bible Roots of Seed Faith

When Abraham got to the place that we know today as Israel, God said, "This is it. This is where you need to settle down." Abraham made his home there, and God began to prosper him. And as time went by, Abraham was greatly prospered.

Then something happened. There was a family squabble. Abraham's nephew Lot and his side of the family decided to break off and go their own way. Instead of getting into a big fight about it, Abraham simply said, "Lot, you choose the land that you want, and I'll take what's left."

Lot chose the well-watered plains of Sodom and Gomorrah, which didn't turn out very well for him. Abraham, however, took the hard scrabble land along the hillside, and God continued to prosper him (Genesis 13:1–18).

But the day came when four kings and their armies came in and kidnapped Lot and all of his people. Abraham sought the Lord and went after them to rescue them from their kidnapping. He defeated the armies and brought Lot and the others back home.

When he arrived, the priest of Salem was there, a man by the name of Melchizedek. Melchizedek came to Abraham with bread and wine, which was a type of holy communion similar to how we take communion today. And then he said something wonderful to Abraham. He said, *Blessed be Abram of God Most High, possessor of heaven and earth; and blessed be God Most High, who has delivered your enemies into your hand* (Genesis 14:19).

When Abraham understood who God was — that God was most high, the possessor of heaven and earth, and the one who delivers him from all of his enemies — he sowed a tithe and an offering. And God established the sowing and reaping principle through Abraham.

Today, we Christians are grafted into the covenant by the faith of Abraham. We look to Abraham as the father of our faith. Abraham obtained knowledge of who God was and what God did for him. And when he did, the Bible says that he began to sow. And God blessed him. God blessed Abraham because he sowed. He is our example of how to give to the Lord in faith.

The One Who Gives You Increase

It is easy to sow seeds in faith when you really understand who God is. Think about who He is for a moment… He loves you. He created you only a little bit lower than the angels (Hebrews 2:7). He's your heavenly Father (Matthew 6:9). He made you in His own image (Genesis 1:27). Greater is He (God) who's in you than he (the devil) that is in the world (1 John 4:4). You can do all things through Christ who strengthens you (Philippians 4:13).

When you understand who God is, you'll *want* to sow into His kingdom. Abraham got a glimpse of what God is like, and that revelation caused him to give.

It also caused him to teach Isaac, his son, to give. And Isaac, the Bible says, learned the lesson so well that he had the courage and faith to sow to the Lord, even during a time of famine.

Even When It Seems Impossible, Increase Can Happen for You

Today, many of us are so far removed from farming and growing our own food that we forget about how all-consuming a famine can be. But I'm sure you can relate to economic downturns, layoffs on the job, struggling bank accounts and situations where it looks like you're in danger of losing all you have. That's what Isaac was facing.

There was a great famine in Isaac's day, according to Genesis 26. At first, Isaac moved to Gerar, where Abimelech the king of the Philistines lived. But things must have looked so bad that Isaac began to think about moving to Egypt. Perhaps he thought there would be food there, or good farmland, or some other answer to his troubles. But God spoke to him and said, "Don't go down to Egypt. Stay here and sow in this land."

Think about it… In the middle of a famine, in the middle of a recession, in the middle of a terrible financial situation, a terrible drought, God said to Isaac, "Stay here, and sow right in the middle of this."

The Bible tells us that Isaac obeyed the word of the Lord. Instead of running away and looking for the world to provide for his needs, he stayed in the land God had given him. He sowed to God in faith, expecting a miracle from God. He trusted God as his source. And the result of his faith and obedience is found in Genesis 26:12–13, which says, *When Isaac planted his crops that year, he harvested a hundred times more grain than he planted, for the Lord blessed him. He became a very rich man, and his wealth continued to grow.* You see, the principle of sowing to God in faith and reaping a harvest from God is biblical, and it works!

Seed Faith Is the God-Kind of Faith

If you open your Bible to Hebrews 11:6, you'll find that it says, *Without faith, it is impossible to please Him* (God). *For he* (or she) *who comes to God must believe that He is a rewarder of those who diligently seek Him.* Without faith, it's impossible to please Him. But when you attach your faith to your seed, it is well-pleasing to God. That's the difference between just throwing money away and *sowing your seed to God.* Your faith must be attached to your giving.

Remember, that's where the phrase *seed faith* comes from. Your faith is attached to your seed. You don't give haphazardly and say, "Well God, I'm just going to throw this at you, and I just wonder if it's ever going to work and help me get out of the situation that I'm in."

No. No, your faith must be attached to the seed you sow. When you attach your faith to your giving, it comes back a sweet smelling sacrifice, acceptable, well-pleasing to God (Philippians 4:18). And because God is a rewarder of those who diligently seek Him, according to Hebrews 11:6, you have a Bible right to expect a harvest from your faith-filled seed sowing. That's what the Bible says. That's unstoppable increase.

Important Points to Remember

1. One of the most powerful examples of someone who lived according to seed-faith principles and prospered because of it was Abraham.
2. When Abraham understood that God was most high, possessor of heaven and earth, and the one who delivered him from his enemies, Abraham was inspired to sow to Him in faith. Likewise, we give to God as a result of understanding who He is in our lives — our provider, our healer, our source for all good things, and our Savior and Lord.
3. It is easy to sow to God in faith when we truly know and believe that He is the one who gives us increase.
4. Even in impossible situations and hard times, God is able to bless us if we will believe Him.
5. Our faith must be attached to the seeds we sow, because it is faith that pleases God and faith that results in our receiving harvests from Him.

Prayer Points

1. Lord, show me daily who You are to me. Reveal Yourself to me in ever increasing ways so that I can come to know You more and more.
2. I trust You to provide me with any increase, harvests and blessings I may need, because You are my Provider and the Source of my increase.
3. Help me to trust fully in You, even when my situation seems impossible to overcome. In spite of how things look, You are always able to work all things together for my good.

Scriptures for Further Study

Genesis 12:1–3
Genesis 13:1–18
Genesis 14:19
Hebrews 2:7
Genesis 1:27
1 John 4:4
Philippians 4:13
Genesis 26:1–6, 12–13
Hebrews 11:6
Philippians 4:18

Chapter 7

The Truth about Tithes and Offerings

"And I will rebuke the devourer for your sakes, so that he will not destroy the fruit of your ground, nor shall the vine fail to bear fruit for you in the field," says the Lord of hosts.

— Malachi 3:11

Many times, people ask me what the Bible really says about tithes and giving offerings. There has been confusion around what God's Word says and what we are asked to do with our finances. Some people believe tithing is only for the Old Testament. Others wonder why you need to give offerings if you're already tithing. If you've ever wondered about the purpose of the tithe and why it matters if you give offerings to the Lord, I pray that this chapter will help answer some of your questions.

The Windows of Blessing Are Wide Open for Those Who Give

The first thing you need to know is that our seeds of faith sown to God are very powerful! When you bring your tithe and offering to the Lord, the Bible says clearly that God will open the windows of heaven, and He'll pour you out a blessing, so much so, there'll not be enough room to receive it. And He'll rebuke the devourer for your sake (Malachi 3:10–11). That's a powerful, life-changing promise!

Why would God have to open windows? Well, you open a window because it's shut, right? Sometimes it can seem as though the windows of blessing are closed tight…as though nothing is going right. But they don't have to stay that way! God can bring increase into your life if you'll obey His Word and act in faith!

One way you can do that is by giving your tithes and offerings to further the work of His kingdom in the earth. "Bring your tithe and offering into the storehouse, into God's work, into God's house," He is saying. "Prove Me, and see if I'll not open you the windows of heaven and pour you out a blessing so great, you won't have enough room to receive it all."

If you study the Bible, you'll only find two mentions of opening the windows of heaven. The first is when God opened the windows of heaven for forty days and forty nights, and it rained (Genesis 7:11). Everything living was destroyed except for Noah, his wife, his family and two of each of the animals that were on the earth at that time. After the Flood, God sent a rainbow and said, "I'll never destroy the earth again by a flood" (Genesis 9:11–13). And He started over again.

The only other time that there's a mention in the Bible of opening the windows of heaven, it's concerning our tithe and our offerings. God said, "I'll open you the windows of heaven and I'll pour you out a blessing so great, you won't be able to contain it." Just like the Flood overwhelmed the earth, the blessings of God will fill your life to the fullest and overflow as you act on His Word and give.

Give God the Opportunity to Bless You

In Malachi 3:8, we find the prophet of God asking a question of the nation of Israel that seems ludicrous when you think about it: *"Will a man rob God?"* You might think that the very idea is ridiculous. How could anyone rob God? Why would anyone want to?

Yet Malachi continues with a shocking revelation: "*Yet you have robbed Me,*" the scripture says. God's people were robbing God! And when you read a little further in that verse, you find out what the problem was. The people were not giving tithes and offerings. They weren't sowing their seeds in faith to the Lord. And as a result, Malachi 3:9 says, "*You are cursed with a curse, for you have robbed Me.*"

The conclusion seems simple, right? Don't rob God. But what does that really mean for today's believer? Why does God say we are robbing Him when we don't give? After all, doesn't He already own all the wealth in the world, all the gold and silver, all the cattle on a thousand hills? Doesn't He already have more than enough?

Of course He does! God doesn't need your money; He doesn't need my money. But He does need our seed sown in faith. And I want to explain what that means for your life, because it's good news.

The answer is found in Malachi 3:10–11, which says, *"Bring all the tithes into the storehouse, that there may be food in My house, and try Me now in this," says the Lord of hosts, "if I will not open for you the windows of heaven and pour out for you* ***such*** blessing *that there will* not *be room* enough *to receive it."*

Did you catch that phrase — *such blessing*? That's why God says we are robbing Him if we don't give in faith. We can't rob God by stealing a $20 bill out of His hands. We can't steal anything from Him. But when we're not acting on our faith in Him by giving to His kingdom and trusting in Him for a harvest, we are robbing God of an opportunity to bless us like only He can do.

When you plant your seed, you put an end to robbing God. That's what happened when the believers at Philippi sent the Apostle Paul an offering while he was in jail in Rome. They knew he was doing the work of God, and they wanted to be a part of it, so they sowed in faith. And as I have already shared, they reaped an amazing promise from God: *And my God shall supply all your need according to His riches in glory by Christ Jesus. Now to our God and Father be glory forever and ever. Amen* (Philippians 4:19–20).

Notice that when we give to God, God not only blesses us with a harvest in return that meets all our need. He also receives glory from the transaction. When He blesses us, He is glorified. Don't rob God of His well-deserved glory by refusing Him opportunities to bless you.

Stop the Devourer in His Tracks

God promises that when we give our tithes and offerings, when we sow in faith, He will rebuke the devourer for our sakes (Malachi 3:11). Who is the devourer? It's the devil, Satan, who comes around for only one reason — to steal, kill, and destroy (John 10:10). Satan is the devourer. When situations arise in our lives that eat away at our health, our finances, or our relationships, that's the devil at work. But God says, "When you give, I will rebuke the devourer. I will rebuke the devil."

What does the word *rebuke* mean? It means, "Stop it! That's enough!" As we give to God in faith, believing for harvests of blessing and expecting Him to meet our needs, He steps in between us and the devil and tells the enemy, "Stop causing trouble! Stop devouring their resources! That's enough!"

Here's an example of the power available to us when God stands between us and the devil. Mark chapter 4 tells of a time that Jesus and His disciples got into a boat to cross the Sea of Galilee. As they sailed, a sudden, violent storm broke out. The situation became so dangerous that the disciples thought they were going to drown. Yet Jesus remained asleep in the back of the boat! They awakened Him and said, "Don't you even care that we're about to drown?"

Well, of course He cared! He wasn't sleeping out of a lack of concern. He simply wasn't fearful of the storm, because He had tremendous faith that God would bring Him safely across the Sea of Galilee. The disciples, though, were in a panic. So, Jesus walked to the front of the boat. He lifted His hands, and the Bible says that He *rebuked* the winds and waves. He essentially said, "Stop it, storm! That's enough!" And there was a great calm (Mark 4:39). The storm ceased at the words of Jesus. He stood between the disciples and the storm and stopped it!

When you bring your tithes and offerings to God, don't be afraid. Even if the circumstances you're facing look bad, don't stay in fear. Trust God to get you through the storms of life. Expect God to open the windows of heaven to you. Expect Him to say to the devourer, the devil, "You stop it! Stop causing trouble for My child. That's enough!" Remember, God protects your seed for you — *as long as you sow it, and sow in faith.*

Sow in Faith Against Your Need

One of the ways we can sow in faith to the Lord is to actively believe that He is meeting our specific, personal needs through His riches in glory by Christ Jesus, just as Philippians 4:19 says. That's how my wife, Lindsay, and I give. When we have specific needs, we tell God about those specific needs, we ask for His help and favor and answers, and then we sow a significant seed into the work of His kingdom. And we stay in faith, believing that God is going to open us the windows of heaven and pour us out the blessing we need.

You can approach your giving and your needs in the same, faith-filled, Bible-based way because it works, no matter what specific need you may have. Maybe the needs are in your family. Maybe they have to do with finances. Or perhaps your needs are in another area of life. Regardless of what you are facing, I encourage you to begin sowing unto the Lord.

Here's one way to do that: Find a good place to sow into — your church, a ministry, a friend who is going on a mission trip, a charity that takes care of widows and orphans, anything that is a way to give in honor of the Lord. As you sow your seed, attach your faith to it and say, "God, this seed represents my faith. I'm sowing this in faith, and I believe in You. I believe Your Word is true. As I sow this seed, I expect You to use it mightily for Your glory, and then multiply it back *good measure, pressed down, shaken together and running over.* In Jesus' name, I pray. Amen."

From that moment forward, praise God and continue to praise Him until the harvest from your seed — the answer to your prayers — arrives.

Never forget this truth: God gives us an opportunity to sow seed *so we can get our needs met.* God doesn't have a need for your money. He's up in heaven. He's walking on streets of gold, in a place where the walls are made of jasper and the gates are made out of pearls (Revelation 21:18–21). He doesn't need our money.

We're the ones who need to sow — *in faith* — so God can use our faith-filled seed and bless it back to us in the way we need it most.

Important Points to Remember

1. Seeds of faith sown to God are very powerful. They open the windows of heaven, allowing for blessings to be poured into our lives.
2. It is possible to rob God of opportunities to bless us by refusing to give tithes and offerings, and failing to sow seeds of faith.
3. When you plant your seed, you put an end to robbing God and put yourself in a position to receive from Him.
4. Sowing our seeds in faith is also a way of stopping the devil from devouring and eating away at what we have.
5. We can take action to turn around needs in our life by sowing seeds to God, acting in faith, and expecting Him to turn things around for our good.

Prayer Points

1. Lord, I bring my needs before you now (name them) and ask You to turn things around in my life for good.
2. Show me any specific seeds I can sow against these needs as an act of my faith in You and Your supply.
3. Help me to stay in faith until the answer to my needs arrives.

Scriptures for Further Study

Malachi 3:8–11
Genesis 7:11
Genesis 9:11–13
Philippians 4:19–20
John 10:10
Mark 4:35–41
Revelation 21:18–21

Chapter 8

How to Ensure a Good Harvest

Let us not grow weary while doing good, for in due season we shall reap if we do not lose heart.

— Galatians 6:9

As you plant seeds to the Lord, there are some things you can do, some strategies to keep in mind and act on, in order to get a good harvest. Think about these things as you sow your seed and as you wait on the Lord for the harvest to come in.

Harvests Come from Good Ground

Jesus told a parable to describe how our seed sowing and harvests work. It's found in Mark chapter 4. In that passage of scripture, the Bible clearly states that you can affect your harvest for good or ill based on where you sow.

For example, when you sow seed onto the "wayside" —

which is an area that has no dirt at all, like a sideway or pavement — the seed can't grow at all, and the birds of the air will come devour it (v. 4). This same parable tells us that you can toss your seed on stony ground (v. 5). The problem with this situation is that stony ground doesn't allow a seed's roots to grow very deep. As soon as harsh conditions come along, like hot sun and a lack of rain, the plant dries up. You can also sow into ground that is filled with thorny weeds. And the weeds and thorns will grow up, choke out your seed, and kill it (v. 7).

So, where do you sow your seed if you want a good harvest? Jesus said to sow it into *good* ground. Mark 4:8 says, *Other seed fell on good ground and yielded a crop that sprang up, increased and produced: some thirtyfold, some sixty, and some a hundred.* When you sow seed into fertile soil, you can expect a good harvest. The Bible even says that the kind of soil you plant in yields a certain kind of return — a thirtyfold, a sixtyfold, even a hundredfold return.

While you can technically sow a seed wherever you want, remember this: some ground is more fertile than others. Some ground is rocky, shallow or hard, but then there's the right ground. I really believe with all my heart that it's very important where we sow seed if we want to see results.

You may ask, "How do I know where to sow? How do I know if the ground is good ground?" God says that if we lack wisdom, we should ask Him and He will give us wisdom (James 1:5). So, if you don't know where to sow your seed, the answer is to pray! If you'll pray, God will show you exactly what to do. He'll show you exactly where to sow and how much to sow.

Personally, I prefer to sow seed where I'm being fed, where I'm getting the teaching of the Word of God, where I'm receiving the prayer of faith. You wouldn't shop at one grocery store, and then pay the bill at a different store. I'm the same way with sowing seed. I like to sow seed into a ministry that I believe in, a ministry that is feeding me.

I encourage you to do the same. Sow into the churches and ministries that are helping you to grow closer to the Lord, and into those that are sharing His saving, healing and delivering power with those in need. God is faithful to give harvests to those who give unto the work of His kingdom.

The Biggest Mistake You Can Make

There are many scriptures throughout the Bible, from Genesis all the way to Revelation, on the subject of sowing and reaping. But to me, the greatest seed faith scripture in the Bible is John 3:16–17, which says, *For God so loved the world that He gave His only begotten Son, that whoever believes in Him should not perish but have everlasting life. For God did not send His Son into the world to condemn the world, but that the world through Him might be saved.* I consider this to be the greatest seed faith passage in the Bible because God made His love an act of His giving.

You know, you can give to someone without loving them, but you cannot love without giving. And God didn't just love. He *so* loved — He loved *so much* — that He gave. And He sowed for a desired result. He sowed so that He might receive something back — you and me!

But the idea that you can give for a desired result goes against what many people have understood. Many Christians have been taught to give, but they have never been taught how to receive. Many have been taught that it is not godly to receive.

Some have taken the scriptures out of context, such as the scripture, *It is more blessed to give than to receive* (Acts 20:35). Some have said it is not good to receive. But the reality is, it is more productive to give than receive, because *only what is given can be multiplied back to you.* If you take nothing and you multiply it, you have nothing left. Zero multiplied by zero equals zero.

So, the biggest mistake Christians can make is not to give at all. And the second biggest mistake is not to expect a harvest from your giving.

Build Up Your Heavenly Account

Another mistake that Christians can make in their seed sowing has to do with what the Apostle Paul tells the church at Philippi about their giving in Philippians 4:17. He said, *Not that I seek the gift, but I seek the fruit that abounds to your account.* Paul was saying that he wasn't seeking gifts from the Philippians for his own good, but for *their* good.

You see, as we give to the Lord in faith, we are laying up treasure in a heavenly account. If you're a seed sower, then you have an account with God. But if you are not a seed sower, you don't have an account with Him. That doesn't mean He doesn't love you or care about you. But it does mean that you haven't given Him your faith in the form of your seed. And as I've already mentioned in this book, without faith it's impossible to please Him.

Rewards...results...harvests... They all come to us through the faith we use actively to reach out to God. No faith and no seed sowing means no harvests. You must sow first, then receive. That is the principle God has set up for giving and receiving.

Many Christians make a related mistake. They give once, then fail to give again. Or they give only once in a while, when they think about it. Maybe they get distracted. Or they worry about their bills. Or they get frustrated because their harvest doesn't come as quickly as they would like. But somehow, for some reason, they don't give regularly. They are not regularly adding to their *heavenly account* with regular acts of faith.

The Philippians gave to Paul once and again (v. 16). They gave over and over. And as a result, God promised to meet their needs with His riches (v. 19). Regular, repeated seed sowing is the way to receive regular, repeated harvests. It's that simple.

Give Your Best Seed, and Do It God's Way

One of the very first offerings we have recorded in the Bible is the offerings that Cain and Abel made to the Lord. And it's a lesson in how to give and how not to give.

Genesis 4:2–5 tells the story of what happened that fateful day:

Now Abel was a keeper of sheep, but Cain was a tiller of the ground. And in the process of time it came to pass that Cain brought an offering of the fruit of the ground to the Lord. Abel also brought of the firstborn of his flock and of their fat. And the Lord respected

Abel and his offering, but He did not respect Cain and his offering. And Cain was very angry, and his countenance fell.

The Bible tells us that Abel gave the firstborn of his sheep unto the Lord, and God received, or accepted, the offering. But Cain gave his offering *in the course of time.* In other words, Cain gave his offering only when he got around to it. And he gave something he wouldn't miss. So, God rejected Cain's half-hearted offering.

The first murder in the Bible happened because Cain got mad that Abel's offering was accepted by God, while his own offering was rejected. Some people might be tempted to think, as Cain apparently did, that God was being unfair. But it is easy to see why Cain's offering was rejected when we consider what God's Word tells us about how to give unto Him.

Jesus made it clear in Luke 6:38 how we are to give to the Lord. He said, *Give, and it will be given to you: good measure, pressed down, shaken together, and running over will be put into your bosom. For with the same measure that you use, it will be measured back to you.* Abel gave with generosity and faith, giving to God the first part of his increase and doing so gladly. Cain did not. Both men received a response back from the Lord in the same spirit with which they gave.

An *acceptable* offering is something that we give according to the Word of God. So what does God's Word say about our offerings?

Exodus 23:19 says, *The first of the firstfruits of your land you shall bring into the house of the Lord your God.* The word *firstfruits* refers to giving the first part of any increase we receive, right off the top. The word *tithe* means tenth, but it also can be translated as "off the top" and "increase."

We are to give to the Lord the first part of our increase, right off the top.

Numbers 18:29 (NIRV) says, *You must bring to the Lord a part of everything given to you. It must be the best and holiest part.* God is not interested in your second-hand handouts. God wants you to give your best — the cream of your crop.

When I was a boy, we lived on a farm, and I sometimes went to milk the cows. It was a lot of fun. We put that raw milk in a refrigerator right there in the barn. And we would come back the next morning and discover that the cream had risen to the top. The best, sweetest part of the milk — the cream — ends up on the top. God wants us to give Him our best — not our worst, but our best seed.

Sowing an offering is not just a good idea; it's an act of obedience to God. We can either obey God's instruction or disobey it. Abel's sacrifice was acceptable because he did it according to the law, the way God set it up. He did it *first.* And he gave his *best.* So he was set up to reap the best. He received God's favor and approval.

Don't Give Up on Your Harvest

Whether I'm out preaching, or teaching on television, or receiving prayer requests from those who write and call in to the Oral Roberts Ministries, one of the most frequent questions I am asked is, "Richard, I've sown my seeds but I haven't received a harvest yet. What do I do if my harvest hasn't come?"

I think the best answer comes from Galatians 6:9, which says, *Let us not grow weary while doing good, for in due season we shall reap if we do not lose heart* — or in other words, if we don't give up.

Here's an example of that principle in action. My mother and I planted a garden when I was a young boy. The first couple of days after planting the seed, I went out to the garden expecting tomatoes, but it wasn't yet tomato time. I was frustrated, to say the least.

But here's the thing I didn't understand at that young age — there was a due season, a time when the tomatoes would be full and ripe and ready for harvest. Until that time, I had to wait on the Lord as Isaiah 40:31 says. *But those who wait on the Lord shall renew their strength; they shall mount up with wings like eagles, they shall run and not be weary, they shall walk and not faint.* I had to wait on God, but guess what? The due season came, and I had many tomatoes to eat.

Imagine what would have happened if I had gone out to that garden day after day, seeing only dirt, and given up on the tomatoes? Even worse, imagine if I had decided to start digging up the dirt because "growing tomatoes doesn't work"? What if I had stopped watering the seeds? I would have missed my harvest! And it would have been my own fault!

Anticipate the Harvest as You Wait

There was a commercial that used to air on television. You see a kid holding a new bottle of ketchup upside down, waiting for the ketchup to come out. And if you've ever used a new bottle of ketchup, you know how long it can take to get it out of the bottle. It seems like it'll take forever.

Sometimes we feel that way about the harvest we are believing God to send us. We ask, "How long do I have to wait for my harvest?" Friend, you wait for it until it comes.

Now, some seed is harvested sooner than others. Why? I don't know. I'm not in charge of the harvest; I don't choose or know the timing. God is in charge of sending the harvest, and He is faithful. So, don't focus on trying to make it all happen on your preferred timeline. Instead, release your faith and believe God to bring about the harvest in His timing, which is always the best timing. Don't try to get ahead of Him. He knows the right moment for that harvest to show up in your life. Trust Him.

One way to wait on the Lord for your harvest is to "water your seed" with your faith. How do you do that? How do you water the seed you've sown in faith to the Lord? You water it by your words, spoken in faith over the seed you have sown. Speak over your seed with words of faith, and don't stop looking for the harvest to come.

Don't speak doubt. Don't say, "This will never work." Don't do that. Use your faith. Make a good confession unto the Lord. Confess that seed is growing in the good soil of the Gospel. Believe that God will open you the windows of heaven and pour you out a blessing. Expect a miracle.

Remember, when it seems like your harvest isn't coming, don't give up. Don't become weary as you do the work and will of the Lord. Hold on, for harvest time is coming. Just as surely as you've sown the seed, the Word of God says the harvest is on its way.

Important Points to Remember

1. It is important to sow into good ground in order to see good harvests. Not all ground is equally good for producing harvests.
2. When you lack wisdom about where to sow your seed, ask God for wisdom according to James 1:5 and act on what He leads you to do.
3. The biggest mistake Christians make is not to sow at all. And the second biggest mistake is failing to expect a harvest from the seeds we sow.
4. Regular, repeated seed sowing is the way to receive regular, repeated harvests.
5. Give God your best seed, the cream of the crop, because that is the way that God has ordained it. And it is through obedience to His ordinances that we receive His harvests.
6. As you wait for your harvest, stay in faith and "water" your seed by praying, praising and speaking good things that are in line with God's Word.

Prayer Points

1. Lord, give me wisdom to know where to plant my seeds of faith. Show me what You consider to be good ground to sow into.
2. You provide seed to the sower (2 Corinthians 9:10), so I ask You to send me seed, and I commit to sowing what You send me.
3. I trust You to provide a good harvest to meet my needs from every seed I have already sown to You. And I praise You for the future harvests that will come from seeds I sow now and in the future, in Jesus' name!

Scriptures for Further Study

Galatians 6:9
Mark 4:1–9
James 1:5
John 3:16–17
Acts 20:35
Philippians 4:16–19
Genesis 4:2–5
Luke 6:38
Exodus 23:19
Numbers 18:29
Isaiah 40:31

Chapter 9

The Blessing Factor

Beloved, I pray that you may prosper in all things and be in health, just as your soul prospers.

— 3 John 2

Everybody wants to be blessed. You want to be blessed; certainly I want to be blessed. So, I want to talk about a biblical principle I like to call the blessing factor. Remember, the law of the harvest is to reap more than you sow. God wants you well in every area of your life. In case it's hard for you to believe God cares whether or not you are prospering, I want to share with you some scriptural reasons that God desires for you to be blessed.

It's His Will to Bless You Abundantly

John 10:10 says, *The thief* (or the devil) *cometh not but for to steal, and to kill and to destroy. But I have come that you might have life and you might have it more abundantly.* Jesus didn't come to give you abundant lack; He came to give you abundant life.

Why? Because it pleases Him! Psalm 35:27 says, *Let them shout for joy and be glad, who favor my righteous cause; and let them say continually, "Let the Lord be magnified, Who has pleasure in the prosperity of His servant."* God wants to bless you because it brings Him pleasure to see you prosper. And pleasing God should be at the top of our daily to-do list. I encourage you not to take it lightly that He is glad when you do well in life.

Deuteronomy 28:11 (AMPCE) says, *And the Lord shall make you have a surplus of prosperity, through the fruit of your body, of your livestock, and of your ground, in the land which the Lord swore to your fathers to give you.* Notice this scripture doesn't say He will give you a surplus of *poverty.* It says He'll give you a surplus of *prosperity.* And this verse even shows a variety of ways in which God can get money to you. Why is He blessing you so abundantly? It's simple. He promised our forefathers to do so, and He keeps His Word. He is not a man that He should lie.

You Can Honor the Lord through Your Finances

Proverbs 3:9–10 (AMPCE) says, *Honor the Lord with your capital and sufficiency [from righteous labors] and with the firstfruits of all your income; so shall your storage places be filled with plenty, and your vats shall be overflowing with new wine.* People are honoring a lot of different things today. But the Bible says, *Honor the Lord.* We honor and glorify Him as we sow to Him, in faith, and as we reap His blessings, in faith.

Notice that these verses talk about *all* of our increase. I believe this is a reminder that you can have multiple streams of income. After all, having many sources of blessings is a great way to experience unstoppable increase in your life! I believe that as we honor God with our best seeds, He will honor us with many sources of blessing and multiple streams of income so we can live the abundant life Jesus has for us.

Financial Blessing Is a Part of God's Covenant with Us

Deuteronomy 8:18 says, *And you shall remember the Lord your God, for it is He who gives you power to get wealth, that He may establish His covenant which He swore to your fathers, as it is this day.* His covenant is that you might be blessed so that you can become a blessing. It's not a dead-end blessing; it's meant to be shared with others. God has given us the power to be rich for a purpose.

Deuteronomy 28:10 (AMPCE) says, *And all people of the earth shall see that you are called by the name [and in the presence of] the Lord, and they shall be afraid of you.* Everybody who comes into contact with you shall know you are a child of God. Now, listen carefully. You cannot be a closet Christian and expect to prosper. You can't be namby-pamby about it. Never be ashamed that you are a servant of the Most High God, the possessor of heaven and earth and the one who delivers you from all of your enemies (Genesis 14:19–20).

We Can Help Fund the Work of His Kingdom

Second Corinthians 8:9 (NIRV) says, *You know the grace shown by our Lord Jesus Christ. Even though he was rich, he became poor to help you. Because he became poor, you can become rich.* These words were written by the apostle Paul, by the inspiration of the Holy Spirit, to the church he established in the city of Corinth. Paul understood it was going to take money to meet the church's needs and allow them to reach out to the lost and hurting of their day.

That same powerful principle continues today. There are hurting people who need our help. There are sick people we must reach with the message of God's healing power. There are lost people who must be reached with the salvation message. All of this takes money to accomplish.

God wants us as Christians to increase so that we can help others as Jesus helps us! Through our seed sowing, we can reach out beyond ourselves and help fund those who are doing the work of the ministry.

Here's a personal example. I found out that a friend of mine has a ministry that reaches out to widows. So, I sent a gift to her to bless those that she blesses. She wrote me back and said, "You don't have any idea what this gift means. I'm currently helping an 85-year-old woman whose husband passed away, and she was about to lose her home due to financial lack. The money you gave will take care of her mortgage payment this month and possibly part of the next month."

It gives me a great blessing to know that I'm helping those in need. James 1:27 (NLT) says, *Pure and genuine religion in the sight of God the Father means caring for orphans and widows in their distress and refusing to let the world corrupt you.* Helping those who are vulnerable and in need, such as widows and orphans, is not optional. Rather, it is an example of Christian love and compassion that we are called to show the world, to draw them to Christ.

Your Entire Life Can Be a Seed

Since I was saved and baptized in the Holy Spirit at the age of 19, the greatest thing I've learned is how to make my life a seed. My love, my time, my money, my prayers, my smiles, a pat on the back, a good word — that's a seed. And God said when I bring that to Him, He will multiply it back and He will bless me so that I might become a blessing.

Because God is no respecter of persons (Acts 10:34), I believe that He wants to bless each of us. He wants to take the seeds we sow to Him, in faith, and return to us a harvest that causes us to increase. From that increase, we can give to Him again, and He can give to us again, and so on and so on in a lifetime cycle of giving and receiving, sowing and reaping! What a glorious promise that is to you and me!

Important Points to Remember

1. Remember, the law of the harvest is to reap more than you sow.
2. It is God's will to bless you abundantly. He didn't come to give you abundant lack; He came to give you abundant life. It pleases Him to see you do well in life.
3. Sowing seeds of our finances into the work of God's kingdom is a powerful way to honor the Lord.
4. God wants us as Christians to increase so that we have the resources to help others in need and share the love of Jesus with them.
5. Our entire lives — everything we have, everything we do, everything we are — can be given as a seed unto the Lord.

Prayer Points

1. According to Your will, Lord, cause me to prosper, increase, and be well in every area of life — spirit, soul, and body.
2. I choose to honor You, Lord, by sowing seeds into Your kingdom.
3. Help me to make my entire life a seed unto You, and help me to share Your love with those in need.

Scriptures for Further Study

3 John 2
John 10:10
Psalm 35:27
Deuteronomy 28:11
Proverbs 3:9–10
Deuteronomy 8:18
Deuteronomy 28:10

Genesis 14:19
2 Corinthians 8:9
James 1:27
Acts 10:34

Chapter 10

The Connection between Blessings and Favor

I will make of you a great nation, and I will bless you [with abundant increase of favors] and make your name famous and distinguished, and you will be a blessing [dispensing good to others].

— Genesis 12:2 (AMPCE)

In Genesis 12:2, God promises Abraham that He will make of him a great nation, blessing him *with abundant increase of favors*. Let this truth get into your spirit: You cannot separate the *blessing* of God from the *favor* of God.

When you study the Bible, you'll see that you don't get one without the other. The blessing of God is an *empowerment* to prosper, to succeed, to multiply, to increase, to excel, and to rise above what attempts to hold you back and keep you down. The favor of God is the *opportunity* to use your abilities to prosper and succeed. Both are needed to help you experience the unstoppable increase God has for you.

Yet many people struggle believing that God wants to bless us and show us favor. Why is that?

The "Problem" with Prosperity

A man once said to me, "Richard, are you a part of that prosperity camp?" Well, I'm certainly not a part of the poverty camp. Maybe that man thought he was being holy by being poor. But that's not what the Bible says. The Bible says that Abraham was rich in cattle, in silver and in gold (Genesis 13:2). It is evident that the blessing and favor of God were on his life. And the Bible says that God is no respecter of persons (Acts 10:34). So, if Abraham could have the blessing and favor of God in his life, then you and I can have them in our lives too.

According to the *Amplified Bible*, the blessing and favor of God made Abraham *extremely rich*. God's blessing has the ability to make a person wealthy and rich in every area of their lives. And yet there are a lot of Christians who have a problem with the idea that Christians can prosper.

I heard my good friend, Jerry Savelle, once say, "There are many Christians who have a problem with Christians being really, truly blessed and becoming rich and wealthy." In my experience, I know there is truth to what he says. There are Christians who look at people in the Bible and say, "Wow, isn't it wonderful that these people in the Bible had all their needs met and had tremendous blessings and tremendous wealth!"

And yet, they also believe it's wrong for Christians today to have it. Why would anyone feel that way? We look at people like Abraham, who in his lifetime was the richest man in his part of the world, and we say we want to be like Abraham in faith. Yet we don't want to have what Abraham had. It just doesn't make any sense to me, especially when God's Word is so clear that He wants to bless us.

I hope by now you are ready to accept the truth that God wants you living an abundant life! Now, let's consider what it takes to truly experience unstoppable increase.

Success Comes from Opportunities

When the blessing of God comes, the favor of God comes with it because they work together to bring about increase in your life. Remember, the blessing is the *empowerment* to prosper, and the favor produces the *opportunity* to prosper. You can have the ability to do something, but if you never have the opportunity, it's not likely the ability is going to bless you.

Imagine, for example, that you can hit a home run every time you come to bat. Or imagine that you can throw a baseball a hundred miles an hour and strike out every batter. Well, that's a blessing, of course. But if you're not ever on a team to stand on a pitcher's mound and throw the ball a hundred miles an hour, or if you never take a bat in your hand, to strike a ball and knock a home run, then the ability doesn't do you much good.

The blessing of God provides a way for the favor of God to open up opportunities that allow you to take the ability you have and bring it into reality. In other words, favor produces opportunity — and opportunity, acted on in faith, can bring about unstoppable increase.

So, here's what I am decreeing by faith over my life, and I encourage you to begin to decree this over your life every day. Say it out loud and make a confession of your faith: "*The blessing of God empowers me to prosper, and the favor of God provides me the opportunities to make it happen.*"

It's Never Too Late

Notice that in the *Amplified* translation of Genesis 12:2, it says *favors* — plural. God has more than one favor to give you — much more than one! If you have ever been given an opportunity and you missed it, don't give up. I believe God is saying, "I'm going to open the door for you to have other opportunities to prosper and to succeed the rest of your life."

Now, how does this happen? It doesn't just happen because you decree something by faith. Your prayers and faith confessions are very important, but you also must act on your faith if you want to receive God's unstoppable increase. And you are to honor God by placing Him first in your life. I used to sing a song on television with these lyrics: "Put Jesus first in your life. Let Him handle the problems that stand in your way." I believe that when you honor God by giving Him first place in your life and trusting in Him, God can place what I call a "commanded blessing" in your life.

What do I mean by that? Well, a "commanded blessing" is a blessing that God commands to come into your life as you honor Him and obey His Word in faith. It's like a magnet. Magnets attract things. When you honor God, then His favor attracts good opportunities and the right people into your life. It attracts new ideas, concepts, insights, and new and innovative ways of doing things. As you honor God, you become a magnet for God's goodness to come into your life.

I believe there are several keys to honoring God in such a way that we position ourselves to receive His blessings and favor. I take these principles from Proverbs 3:1–10.

Obey the Word of the Lord

The first principle of obtaining God's favor is *obedience.* Proverbs 3:1–2 (NIRV) says, *My son, do not forget my teaching. Keep my commands in your heart. They will help you live for many years. They will bring you peace and success.* In order to practice obedience to God's Word, we must first know what His Word says. You can't practice something that you don't know. As we read the Bible and learn more about God, we can begin to keep His commandments in our hearts and get better and better at obeying Him.

As we're obedient to God's Word, we grow in Him. As we act in faith as Proverbs 3:1 says, then the promise in Proverbs 3:2 comes into play. Success and peace aren't just accidental; they are blessings that result from our willingness to do what God says and to live according to His ways.

Living in Integrity with Others

The next key to obtaining God's favor is *integrity*. Proverbs 3:3–4 (NIRV) says, *Don't let love and truth ever leave you. Tie them around your neck. Write them on the tablet of your heart. Then you will find favor and a good name in the eyes of God and people.* Our obedience to God's Word is deeply connected to our integrity, especially in how we behave in relation to other people.

Integrity is defined as "the quality of being honest and having strong moral principles; moral uprightness." And it is a crucial part of walking in abundance because our relationships are more important than anything else in our lives. Jobs come and go. Successes may come and go. But our relationships with God and other people are key to our existence, and living honestly and morally is a key to maintaining healthy relationships.

When you and I act in love and faithfulness, then we build integrity and we positively impact our relationships. And as a result, we win favor and a good name in the sight of God and people.

Keep Trusting in God

A third way to position ourselves for success with God and people is to *trust* God. Proverbs 3:5–6 (NIRV) says, *Trust in the Lord with all your heart. Do not depend on your own understanding. In all your ways obey Him. Then He will make your paths smooth and straight.*

So often, we try to figure everything out; we get too analytical. But some things cannot be understood with our natural minds. Instead, they must be taken on faith. So, we must learn to trust God with all our heart and lean not on our own understanding. We can lean on Him in everything we do. We can turn to Him for His ideas, instead of just trying to make things work based on our own ideas.

Our ideas may be good ideas, but they might not be God's best idea for us. Often, He has a plan that is far, far better than we can dream up ourselves — we just need to trust Him and be open to His plans. And in the long run, it's always better to go His way, because He sees the path ahead of us and knows what obstacles we need to avoid.

Resist Sin and Avoid Wrongdoing

Fourth, if you want to experience God's favor, you must draw on your God-given ability to *discern* wrongdoing and errors. Proverbs 3:7–8 (NIRV) says, *Don't be wise in your own eyes. Have respect for the Lord and avoid evil. That will bring health to your body. It will make your bones strong.*

God has given us, through His Word and the Holy Spirit, the ability to identify right from wrong. And that ability is essential to our success in life, because it can direct us toward what is good for us and away from troubles.

Simply put, godly discernment is that little inward voice that speaks to you and tells you, "Stay away from this. Move toward this." As we listen to the Lord and follow His wise inward voice, we can avoid the mistakes that would disrupt our harvests, and we can keep moving toward abundance.

Honor God with What You Possess

I've said this before, but I'll say it again because it's so important. We are to give God our best. Proverbs 3:9–10 (NIRV) says, *Honor the Lord with your wealth. Give him the first share of all your crops. Then your storerooms will be so full they can't hold everything. Your huge jars will spill over with fresh wine.*

Now, your *crops* are your resources — your time, your talent, your love — all the things that you produce in your life. When you give God the *first share of all your crops* (your firstfruits), you are giving Him your best, not your second-best and certainly not your worst. We are not to give something to God that doesn't mean anything to us, because when we give Him something that doesn't mean anything to us, then it won't mean anything to Him either.

We're to give Him our best in terms of our time, our money, and our talent. As we maintain a generous heart to give, God can take our gift, use it for His glory, and multiply it back to us in a harvest that fills us to overflowing.

Expect God's Abundance in Your Life

No matter how well and faithfully you live according to these principles, there's a final step to remember — *expect your miracle.* As you sow to God in faith, continue to live as Proverbs 3 exhorts you to live. Be a person of integrity and honor. Be a person who discerns right from wrong. Be someone who lives according to the truth of God's Word. Continually give God first place in your life. As you do this on a committed, regular basis, as part of how you live every moment of your life, I believe that God's blessing and favor will surely be manifested in your life.

Important Points to Remember

1. You cannot separate the blessing of God from the favor of God. Both are necessary to help you experience the unstoppable increase that God has for you.
2. The blessing of God is an empowerment to prosper, succeed, multiply, increase, excel and rise above anything that attempts to hold you back.
3. The favor of God is the opportunity to use your abilities to prosper and succeed.
4. These opportunities, when acted on in faith, can bring about increase in your life.
5. It is never too late to be blessed and experience God's provision.
6. Keys to obtaining God's favor include obeying the Lord, living in integrity, trusting God, avoiding sin and wrongdoing, honoring God with what you have, and expecting His blessings.

Prayer Points

1. Lord, empower me to prosper in all I do for You.
2. Provide me with opportunities to use the abilities You have given me. And help me to take advantage of those opportunities by faith, so that they can bring about harvests for me.
3. If I have missed out on or neglected any opportunities You have given me in the past, forgive me and help me to move forward in alignment with Your will for my life.
4. Help me daily to obey You, live with integrity, trust You, avoid wrongdoing, honor You, and expect Your blessings.

Scriptures for Further Study

Genesis 12:2
Genesis 13:2
Acts 10:34
Proverbs 3:1–10

Chapter 11

The Blessings that Come to Those Who Sow

Honor the Lord with your wealth. Give him the first share of all your crops. Then your storerooms will be so full they can't hold everything. Your huge jars will spill over with fresh wine.

— Proverbs 3:9–10 (NIRV)

At the beginning of this book, I told you how the Lord spoke to me during my prayer time and how He said to me: "I'm bringing seven new seasons into the life of those who will sow."

Now that you have read and considered how God works through our seed-sowing, and how we can honor Him with the increase of our resources and what the true purpose of money is, we can consider in more detail what God means when He says He is bringing about seven new seasons for those who sow.

These are the blessings of unstoppable increase that I believe God is bringing into your life as you commit yourself to continually giving to His kingdom in faith, generously and joyfully, expecting miracles. And these are the blessings I am praying and believing God to bring about for you right now.

A Season of Abundance

I believe God is bringing those who sow into a season of abundance. The definition of the word *abundance* literally means "great plenty, overflowing quantity, and ample sufficiency." John 10:10 (KJV) says, *The thief* [or the devil] *cometh not but for to steal, and to kill, and to destroy.* Satan has an agenda to steal from you, to kill you, and to destroy you. But don't stop there! The rest of the scripture says, *But I* [Jesus] *have come that you might have life, and that you might have it more abundantly.* God wants you to have an abundant life, with more than enough to meet your needs and give to others.

Maybe you have faced difficulties. Perhaps you're in a faith fight with your enemy, the devil. Yes, the devil wants to separate you from your faith, for if he is successful at separating you from your faith, then he has you. But you can set your faith as a sower and believe God for His abundance in your life.

Remember, God is faithful. When it looks like your situation is at its darkest, that's when the Lord shows up with a mighty, mighty victory!

A Season of Joy

The Bible speaks of joy unspeakable and full of glory (1 Peter 1:8). There is a supernatural season of indescribable, overwhelming, glorious joy coming into the life of the sower.

This is good news, especially because as we live in this world, we can often face situations that result in sorrow, pain, disappointments, depression, fear and loneliness. We need the joy of the Lord to make it through such times.

Jesus Himself said in John 16:20, *Your grief will turn to joy.* Joy replaces misery, but sometimes we have to step out in faith to believe for it. If you will sow to the Lord in faith, He is ready to turn your captivity into laughter and joy. The days of mourning are over. It is time for the joy of the Lord, which is our strength (Nehemiah 8:10).

A Season of Peace

I was watching an interview with a great Hollywood actor on the news, and at the end of the interview, the newsperson said, "With all the success you've had, all the awards you've won, and all the money you've made, what is it that you don't have?" The actor looked down and said, "I don't have peace."

There's something powerful and healing about having peace in your life. I'm not talking about the kind of peace that the world brings. I'm talking about the peace of God that passes all understanding (Philippians 4:7), the kind of peace that helps you sleep at night. When we have peace, we are without stress, and we are assured in our security. Yes, you may have been through some battles or struggles, but as you sow to God in faith, I believe a season of peace is coming, and according to Romans 16:20, *The God of peace will soon crush the devil under your feet.* That is a Bible promise.

A Season of Favor

You'll find in Luke 2:52 that Jesus grew in wisdom and in stature and in favor with God and people. As you sow, I believe you can expect the Lord to bring a new season of favor into your life. Remember, favor is acceptance. It's approval. It opens doors. Favor gives you an advantage. It causes hardened hearts to soften and become tender toward you. Expect to see the favor of the Lord opening up doors of opportunity and promotion for you as you sow.

A Season of Harvest

A farmer's happiest time is when he's sowing, because he knows harvest time will come.

Some of you have planted seed, but you have not yet reaped the harvest. I'm telling you on the authority of the Word of God, *Let us not grow weary while doing good, for in due season we shall reap if we do not lose heart* (Galatians 6:9). That means don't give up. Don't stop planting your seeds, and don't stop believing. There is a harvest time for you as you continue to sow and continue to believe God for His increase and abundance.

A Season of Power

Many people today have experienced a season of enduring the attacks of the devil and all those who are doing his bidding. The devil may have shown his power against you, but I believe as you sow, the Lord will bring you into a season of experiencing the mighty power of God to destroy the works of the devil. I'm reminded of the scripture in 1 John 3:8, *For this purpose the Son of God was manifested, that He might destroy the works of the devil.* We are empowered by the Holy Spirit to bring deliverance to the captives. I believe He will work with us and confirm His Word with miracles, signs, and wonders following.

A Season of Intimacy with the Lord

Many Christians have become lukewarm in their relationship with God. Lukewarm is described as being neither hot nor cold, and we are to be hot, passionate, zealous for the Lord. Thankfully, as we repent for being lukewarm, then according to 1 John 1:9, *God is faithful and just to forgive us of our sins, and to cleanse us of all unrighteousness.* As we repent of our sins, failures, and wrongdoings, the Lord draws close to us, and we can have that renewal of intimacy with Him.

In Psalm 139:23–24, David said, *Search me, O God, and know my heart; try me, and know my anxieties; and see if there is any wicked way in me, and lead me in the way everlasting.* This is a constant thing that we Christians need to do in order to maintain a close, intimate walk with the Lord. In fact, David was called a man after God's own heart, because he did this self-examination of himself regularly every day. And God was with him because of it.

Don't Hold Back

With all my heart today, I urge you to begin to sow, if you're not already a sower.

If you're already a sower, I encourage you to sow regularly and sincerely, not haphazardly. Don't say, "Well, I'll sow this month, then I'll skip two or three months." No, no, no! Be a regular sower.

If you sow regularly, I encourage you to continue to do what you're already doing. Continue to sow in faith into the good soil of the Gospel. And when you sow, say, "God, I'm sowing this into the good soil of the Gospel. Use it for your glory, and then multiply it back as you said in Luke 6:38, *good measure, pressed down, shaken together and running over.*"

Be a sower, and allow God to bring these seven new seasons in your life.

Important Points to Remember

1. As we sow in faith to the Lord, we can expect to experience an abundant life with more than enough to meet our needs and bless others.
2. As we sow in faith, we can expect joy unspeakable and full of glory.
3. As we sow in faith, we can expect the peace of God, which surpasses all understanding and guards our hearts and minds.
4. As we sow in faith, we can expect to have favor with God and with people, bringing about open doors to new opportunities.
5. As we sow in faith, we can expect to receive harvests from the seeds we sow.
6. As we sow in faith, we can expect the power of God to fill our lives, bringing about deliverance and miracles, and defeating the work of the devil.
7. As we sow in faith, we can expect to experience intimacy and closeness with the Lord.

Prayer Points

1. Lord, thank You for Your seasons of blessings as I sow unto You in faith. Thank You for abundance, joy, peace, favor, harvests, power, and intimacy with You.
2. I commit to giving You my whole heart, putting my faith into my giving. I will not hold back in sowing my seeds to You.

Scriptures for Further Study

Proverbs 3:9–10
John 10:10

1 Peter 1:8
John 16:20
Nehemiah 8:10
Philippians 4:7
Romans 16:20
Luke 2:52
Galatians 6:9
1 John 3:8
1 John 1:9
Psalm 139:23–24
Luke 6:38

Epilogue

My Prayer for You

For surely there is a hereafter, and
your hope will not be cut off.

— Proverbs 23:18

All of these blessings and so much more are available to you through your faith in the Lord, especially as you commit yourself to walking in the principles of seed faith, giving and receiving, and unstoppable increase that are contained in this book.

So, begin to rejoice that God has more for you in every area of your life, and begin to act in faith from what you have learned through what you have read. And as you do, I believe God will bring His unstoppable increase into your life.

And now, I want to pray for you...

Right now, in the authority of Jesus' mighty name, I pray over you as you are reading this very special message. I pray that there would be an excitement in your heart, a new zeal to serve God like never before. I pray that you will come into agreement with God in your giving, and that you will act in faith to bring these seven new seasons into your life by sowing, by sowing unto the Lord. And I prophesy today what the Bible says. If you'll do it, God will begin to bring these seven new seasons into your life. I pray this in faith, and I believe it with all my heart, and I am expecting God to multiply every seed that you sow, and bring these seven new seasons to the forefront of your life. In Jesus' mighty name, amen and amen. Hallelujah. Praise the Lord!

Scriptures of Abundance and Increase for You

As you sow your seed, believing for and expecting miracles of increase and abundance in your life, let these scriptures build you up and give you a focus for your prayers and your faith.

Genesis 8:22 NKJV

While the earth remains, seedtime and harvest, cold and heat, winter and summer, and day and night shall not cease.

Exodus 25:2 NKJV

Speak to the children of Israel, that they bring Me an offering. From everyone who gives it willingly with his heart you shall take My offering.

Deuteronomy 8:18 NIV

But remember the Lord your God, for it is he who gives you the ability to produce wealth, and so confirms his covenant, which he swore to your ancestors, as it is today.

Deuteronomy 28:2–13 NIV

All these blessings will come on you and accompany you if you obey the Lord your God: You will be blessed in the city and blessed in the country. The fruit of your womb will be blessed, and the crops of your land and the young of your livestock—the calves of your herds and the lambs of your flocks. Your basket and your kneading trough will be blessed. You will be blessed when you come in and blessed when you go out. The Lord will grant that the enemies who rise up against you will be defeated before you. They will come at you from one direction but flee from you in seven. The Lord will send a blessing on your barns and on everything you put your hand to. The Lord your God will bless you in the land he is giving you. The Lord will establish you as his holy people, as he promised you on oath, if you keep the commands of the Lord your God and walk in obedience to him. Then all the peoples on earth will see that you are called by the name of the Lord, and they will fear you. The Lord will grant you abundant prosperity — in the fruit of your womb, the young of your livestock and the crops of your ground — in the land he swore to your ancestors to give you. The Lord will open the heavens, the storehouse of his bounty, to send rain on your land in season and to bless all the work of your hands. You will lend to many nations but will borrow from none. The Lord will make you the head, not the tail. If you pay attention to the commands of the Lord your God that I give you this day and carefully follow them, you will always be at the top, never at the bottom.

Joshua 1:8 NLT

Study this Book of Instruction continually. Meditate on it day and night so you will be sure to obey everything written in it. Only then will you prosper and succeed in all you do.

Job 36:11 NIV

If (you) *obey and serve Him,* (you) *will spend the rest of* (your) *days in prosperity and* (your) *years in contentment.*

Psalm 5:12 NLT

For you bless the godly, O Lord; you surround them with your shield of love.

Psalm 23:1 NIV

The Lord is my shepherd, I lack nothing.

Psalm 34:10 NIV

The lions may grow weak and hungry, but those who seek the Lord lack no good thing.

Psalm 35:27 NKJV

Let the Lord be magnified, Who has pleasure in the prosperity of His servant.

Psalm 37:3–4 NLT

Trust in the Lord and do good. Then you will live safely in the land and prosper. Take delight in the Lord, and he will give you your heart's desires.

Psalm 37:25–26 NIV

I was young and now I am old, yet I have never seen the righteous forsaken or their children begging bread. They are always generous and lend freely; their children will be a blessing.

Psalm 50:10 NKJV

For every beast of the forest is Mine, and the cattle on a thousand hills.

Psalm 68:19 NKJV

Blessed be the Lord, Who daily loads us with benefits, the God of our salvation!

Psalm 103:2–5 NKJV

Bless the Lord, O my soul, and forget not all His benefits: who forgives all your iniquities, who heals all your diseases, who redeems your life from destruction, who crowns you with lovingkindness and tender mercies, who satisfies your mouth with good things, so that your youth is renewed like the eagle's.

Proverbs 3:9–10 NKJV

Honor the Lord with your possessions, and with the firstfruits of all your increase; so your barns will be filled with plenty, and your vats will overflow with new wine.

Proverbs 8:12 KJV

I dwell with prudence, and find out knowledge of witty inventions.

Proverbs 10:4 NIV

Lazy hands make for poverty, but diligent hands bring wealth.

Proverbs 11:25 NKJV

The generous soul will be made rich, and he who waters will also be watered himself.

Proverbs 13:22 NKJV

A good man leaves an inheritance to his children's children, but the wealth of the sinner is stored up for the righteous.

Isaiah 48:17 AMPCE

Thus says the Lord, your Redeemer, the Holy One of Israel: I am the Lord your God, Who teaches you to profit, Who leads you in the way that you should go.

Jeremiah 7:23 NLT

This is what I told them: 'Obey me, and I will be your God, and you will be my people. Do everything as I say, and all will be well!'

Malachi 3:10–11 NKJV

"Bring all the tithes into the storehouse, that there may be food in My house, and try Me now in this," says the Lord of hosts, "if I will not open for you the windows of heaven and pour out for you such blessing that there will not be room enough to receive it. And I will rebuke the devourer for your sakes, so that he will not destroy the fruit of your ground, nor shall the vine fail to bear fruit for you in the field," says the Lord of hosts.

Haggai 2:8 NKJV

"The silver is Mine, and the gold is Mine," says the Lord of hosts.

Matthew 5:6 NKJV

Blessed are those who hunger and thirst for righteousness, for they shall be filled.

Matthew 6:31–33 NKJV

Therefore do not worry, saying, "What shall we eat?" or "What shall we drink?" or "What shall we wear?" For after all these things the Gentiles seek. For your heavenly Father knows that you need all these things. But seek first the kingdom of God and His righteousness, and all these things shall be added to you.

Matthew 19:29 NKJV

And everyone who has left houses or brothers or sisters or father or mother or wife or children or lands, for My name's sake, shall receive a hundredfold, and inherit eternal life.

Matthew 21:22 NIV

If you believe, you will receive whatever you ask for in prayer.

Luke 6:38 NKJV

Give, and it will be given to you: good measure, pressed down, shaken together, and running over will be put into your bosom. For with the same measure that you use, it will be measured back to you.

John 10:10 NIV

The thief comes only to steal and kill and destroy; I have come that they may have life, and have it to the full.

John 16:24 NIV

Until now you have not asked for anything in my name. Ask and you will receive, and your joy will be complete.

Romans 8:32 MSG

If God didn't hesitate to put everything on the line for us, embracing our condition and exposing himself to the worst by sending his own Son, is there anything else he wouldn't gladly and freely do for us?

Romans 8:37 NLT

Despite all these things, overwhelming victory is ours through Christ, who loved us.

2 Corinthians 9:6–11 NIV

Remember this: Whoever sows sparingly will also reap sparingly, and whoever sows generously will also reap generously. Each of you should give what you have decided in your heart to give, not reluctantly or under compulsion, for God loves a cheerful giver. And God is able to bless you abundantly, so that in all things at all times, having all that you need, you will abound in every good work. As it is written: "They have freely scattered their gifts to the poor; their righteousness endures forever." Now he who supplies seed to the sower and bread for food will also supply and increase your store of seed and will enlarge the harvest of your righteousness. You will be enriched in every way so that you can be generous on every occasion, and through us your generosity will result in thanksgiving to God.

Galatians 6:7,9 NKJV

Do not be deceived, God is not mocked; for whatever a man sows, that he will also reap… And let us not grow weary while doing good, for in due season we shall reap if we do not lose heart.

Ephesians 1:3 NLT

All praise to God, the Father of our Lord Jesus Christ, who has blessed us with every spiritual blessing in the heavenly realms because we are united with Christ.

Philippians 4:19 NIV

And my God will meet all your needs according to the riches of his glory in Christ Jesus.

Colossians 3:23–24 NKJV

And whatever you do, do it heartily, as to the Lord and not to men, knowing that from the Lord you will receive the reward of the inheritance; for you serve the Lord Christ.

James 1:17 NIV

Every good and perfect gift is from above, coming down from the Father of the heavenly lights, who does not change like shifting shadows.

James 4:7 KJV

Submit yourselves therefore to God. Resist the devil, and he will flee from you.

1 John 5:14 NKJV

Now this is the confidence that we have in Him, that if we ask anything according to His will, He hears us.

3 John 2 KJV

Beloved, I wish above all things that thou mayest prosper and be in health, even as thy soul prospereth.

The History Behind the Concept of Seed Faith

as Told by Oral Roberts

My father, Oral Roberts, often told the story of how God first revealed to him the biblical principle of giving and receiving, seed time and harvest, that Dad called seed faith. If you've never heard it before, here is my father's story — in his own words.

—Richard

At the beginning of my ministry, just prior to my entering the healing ministry, my wife, Evelyn, and I were facing a terrible need in our lives. We had just moved to Enid, Oklahoma, where I was to pastor a small church and attend college while making $55 per week as my salary from the church. The church didn't have a place for us to live, and when I went to the church board for help, *I couldn't get anywhere with them!*

Fortunately, a member of the church took mercy on us and invited Evelyn and me and our two children to stay with them. Can you imagine two families with several children living in a two-bedroom house that had only about a thousand square feet?

One day Evelyn had had enough, and she poured out her frustration about it to me. She said, "Oral, if you don't get these children and me a place to live, I'm going home to my mother, and I'm not coming back until you get me a house." Let me tell you, that got me into motion!

That night, I went to our prayer meeting with a new anointing. I don't remember everything I preached about, but it was hotter than fire.

The Lord brought Malachi 3:10–11 to me, which states that if you bring your tithes and offerings into His storehouse, He will open the windows of heaven and pour you out a blessing where there is not room enough to contain it. And, oh, how I needed a blessing!

At the end of the service, I experienced a strong leading from the Holy Spirit to try to raise the down payment for a parsonage for our church. The Lord spoke in my spirit and said, "Take your week's salary and lay it on the altar at the front of the sanctuary, and you start the giving." Now, He was talking about my whole $55 paycheck.

I told the congregation, "We're taking up an offering for a down payment on a parsonage for the pastor — not only for me but also for any pastor who follows me." Then I laid

ORAL ROBERTS

down my paycheck and said, "Who else would like to give?"

To my absolute astonishment, people popped up everywhere! I mean, people began giving $100 and $20 and other amounts, and the wealthiest man in the church gave $1,000. When the meeting was over, I had the down payment on a parsonage. And the church felt good about taking care of the pastor — any pastor — rather than seeing him and his family nearly starving to death.

After I got home that night, Evelyn asked me how the service went, and I said, "It was good. Wonderful things happened."

"Like what?" she asked.

"I raised the down payment on a parsonage," I replied.

She was shocked as she almost whispered, "How much did *you* give?"

"I gave the best I could — our week's salary."

"You didn't give the whole thing!" she cried. "How am I going to buy groceries for our children this week?"

"Honey, I don't know, but the Lord told me to do it, so I did it."

Around four o'clock in the morning, we were awakened by a loud knock on the door. I ran to open it and found Art Newfield, a man from the church, standing there. He was one of the largest wheat farmers in northwestern Oklahoma.

He apologized for coming by and waking me up so early. Then he said, "Brother Roberts, I was at the service last night, but I didn't give any money for the new parsonage. I went home and went to bed, but I couldn't sleep. An hour ago, I got up and went out into the yard and dug this up."

Then he laid four $100 bills in my hand. I had never had a $100 bill in my hand before. Now he was handing me seven times more than I had given in the offering that night to build a parsonage for the church. My $55 had become seven times more!

But the greatest revelation of all came next when Art said to me, "I want to tell you why I gave you this money. As you know, I'm a wheat farmer, and I know I have to plant a seed to get a harvest in my wheat field. This $400 is not just money. It's a seed of my faith I am sowing to the Lord to get my own needs met."

When he spoke those words, something went off inside my spirit! There was a moment when everything in me stood still, and my spirit man leaped as it connected with this divine principle from God.

I was raised on a farm for the first fourteen years of my life, and I had helped my father plant corn and cotton every year. I knew what it was to plant and reap a harvest, but I had never associated this principle with the realm of faith until this day.

Seed Faith in Action

True Stories from People who Received God's Increase

I pray these testimonies on God's faithfulness to bring about increase from seed sowing inspire you to test Him yourself and see that He indeed opens the windows of heaven to those who give to Him in faith!

Everything Fell Apart, but God Turned It Around

While in college, I would often see Richard and Lindsay Roberts on their TV program, *The Place for Miracles*. Through their teaching on seed faith giving, I was led to sow seeds into the Oral Roberts Ministries. At the time, I was a vice principal at a charter school, with a lovely home, family and nice cars.

But suddenly, everything fell apart. Eventually, I found myself with no place to go. I didn't have 50 cents to my name. But while packing up to leave my friend's house, I found a $100 bill. I just knew I had to sow it into the Oral Roberts Ministries for a miracle.

Soon, a friend from out of state called and blessed me with $5,000! And now, I have a place to live and a car, and I get to keep my son for the summer. My son is planning to go to law school. It's a blessing.

I would say to everyone going through tough times — believe, stay in faith, and watch God work it out. He will watch over His Word to make sure it is performed. And thank God for Richard and Lindsay, and for the Oral Roberts Ministries and its awesome Abundant Life Prayer Group. Thanks for being there for me!

Reginald from Georgia

God Is Healing My Friends and Prospering My Business

I called the Abundant Life Prayer Group after my friend, Frances, had a stroke. Frances was unable to walk and was in a nursing home getting bed sores. It was not good.

I decided to begin sowing seeds into your ministry that week. Frances's condition continued to improve, and I continued to call the prayer line each week. As I continued to stay in prayer and sow seeds of faith, Frances improved until she was completely healed and was able to leave the nursing home.

Also, I asked the prayer partners to pray for the success of my business. As I continued to sow my seeds, my telephone business began to make more money each month. My income went up almost every month, and I was able to increase the amount I was sowing. Within a year, my business doubled! Our prayers and tithing and alms-giving really work! Praise Jesus!

Joe from Texas

Prayer Cloth and Seed Faith Delivered Our Daughter!

Our daughter, Sarah Grace, received a miracle of healing, and we feel it is due to the seed faith teaching of the Roberts family.

Our journey began with a prenatal ultrasound. Doctors examined the results and became concerned that our baby's right kidney might be cystic. We battled in prayer for a miracle with our church and with the Abundant Life Prayer Group. In the next ultrasound, no kidney problems showed up. But there was a possible umbilical cord hernia preventing proper nutrition to our baby.

When my wife Glenda's water broke, we went to the hospital, where they had to induce her labor. Baby Sarah's heartbeat slowed to nearly zero with every contraction. An emergency C-section was performed. Her very birth was a miracle!

Hours later, to our shock and dismay, Sarah had to be transported to a special children's hospital. Doctors ruled out the possible umbilical cord hernia, which would have required surgery. But a CT scan showed she had enlarged ventricles of the brain. This can lead to pressure on the brain, resulting in neurological problems if not treated quickly through surgery.

Sarah was placed in an incubator in NICU. At first, her condition grew worse. She developed infant diabetes that wasn't responding to insulin. Surgery to relieve the pressure on her brain was scheduled.

We put a prayer cloth from your ministry in Sarah's diaper right before she went into surgery. We felt this point of contact, along with prayer, would be a major factor in her outcome. And it was. The surgery went fine, and the diabetes became regulated and stabilized.

While we waited for Sarah to recover, I was walking and praying — and I found $15 on the ground. There was no one there who could have lost it. Immediately, the Oral Roberts Ministries came to mind. My wife and I prayed over the money and sowed it as a seed of faith that God had our situation in His hands.

At the time, a nurse told us that Sarah's blood count was too low and that she might need a blood transfusion. But three days later, Sarah's condition improved and she was moved out of NICU and into a regular room.

From that point on, Sarah continued to get better. She had two more surgeries to deal with the enlarged brain ventricles and had some continued treatments for infant diabetes. By the time she was 7 months old, the diabetes was gone. She is now 12 years old and doing well. Hallelujah!

Kenneth from Alabama

Jobs, Jobs, Jobs!

Both of my daughters lost their jobs within weeks of each other. At the time, I had begun watching *The Place for Miracles.* And I heard Richard praying for people to receive jobs.

I got really excited, and I started listening very closely to what he said. Then I prayed in faith and agreement with him. Also, as a point of contact to release my faith for miracles, I sowed a seed into the Oral Roberts Ministries and believed that God would enable both of my daughters to get new jobs. I didn't have much, but I sowed what I had.

The following week, my oldest daughter had interviews set up for two different companies. While she was in one of those interviews, a third company called and left her a message in response to her resume. She received a job offer today for the job she really wanted, and it paid the maximum salary for her position. She is making $10,000 more a year than she did when she left her other job.

My youngest daughter received an interview too, and she is waiting for confirmation, but she is very confident that she's going to get this job.

As a matter of fact, I got a job in the meanwhile as well. Thank you for your ministry and prayer. I am learning a lot from you!

Rhonda from Tennessee

Praying and Seed Sowing Has Changed My Life

I'm always telling my coworkers, family, friends, and neighbors about the Abundant Life Prayer Group. I tell them how praying with you has changed my life and given me great confidence as I stand face to face with life's challenges.

When I first called you in 2007 for prayer, I was ready to give up because I could not find a way to get a car. My aunt suggested I call and pray in agreement with the Abundant Life Prayer Group for a miracle. That prayer was answered.

Since then, I've prayed in agreement with the Prayer Group and seen God meet my needs in many ways. He has provided me with an apartment, jobs, bills taken care of, unexpected money, furniture, food, health and more.

Recently when my job was terminated, I called the Abundant Life Prayer Group to agree in prayer and sowed my seed in faith, believing for a new full-time job with good benefits, in a good location. And that's exactly what I received — a job with good benefits in a beautiful location. The position I was hired for is even better than the one I initially applied for.

No one could ever love me the way Jesus does! I thank Him for giving me the desires of my heart.

Andrew from Florida

"Avalanche" of Miracles

Recently, I sowed a seed faith gift into the Oral Roberts Ministries as a point of contact to release my faith for a financial need to be met. I was asking God for a dependable automobile, as the one I was driving at the time kept breaking down. I was even forced to stop driving that vehicle for seven weeks, leaving me without transportation.

So, I spoke with my husband and we agreed to sow in

faith for a new vehicle — a good ride. I sowed our seed and released my faith.

A month or so after we planted this seed and believed God for a harvest, I received a call from a family member who had gotten a financial increase. They asked me to meet them at a car dealership so I could pick out a new car or truck, and they would pay for it.

I was in awe! I knew immediately that God had answered my prayer. Now, I am driving a new Chevy Avalanche truck — and it's totally paid for. God is so awesome! He gets all the glory for this miracle.

Charlene from North Carolina

Giving to God Reversed Our Financial Woes

About a year ago, things began to get tight financially. My wife, Arleen, and I decided we were going to increase our giving to the Oral Roberts Ministries. Our church had financial problems, and I was working part-time. When Richard began to preach a message about the God Who is "more than enough," I took that to heart. And I preached that way to my church as well.

Long story short, we got what for my church is a very large gift of $78,000 from someone who died. It was in the will and there are no restrictions on it. For our church, that gift amounts to almost an entire year's budget. God says in Malachi 3:10–11, "Just try Me. Just test Me, and prove Me that when you give, I'll open the windows of heaven to you." You can never out-give God.

Pastor Cyril from Oregon

Seed Faith Giving and Living Eliminates Massive Debt!

A few years ago, my wife and I decided to give our lives completely to the Lord. I quit a good job and began working for a much smaller salary. Money was scarce, and before I knew it, I had a $13,000 credit card debt. We needed a miracle.

We asked the Lord's forgiveness for trying to do things our way, and we began tithing. Through the Oral Roberts Ministries, we learned about seed faith living, and we began paying off the debt we owed. We were also led by the Lord to sow seed into the Oral Roberts Ministries. I soon got a good job, and a small inheritance we received let us pay off the remaining credit card debt, plus give tithes and sow more seed.

Through more resources from the Oral Roberts Ministries, I learned that seed faith isn't just about sowing money, but it's a way of life, which includes sowing seeds of forgiveness. After learning that, I wrote a letter of apology to someone. As soon as it was mailed, we received a call from our realtor with an offer for our home, which was for sale. I immediately planted a seed into your ministry, and we got $5,000 more than we expected on the counteroffer for our home, which helped us pay off more bills!

Except for our current house — which has a mortgage $20,000 less than our old one — we are now debt-free! My wife quit work and is home with our children. We serve an awesome God!

Michael from Florida

Consistent Giving Leads to New House

I have been praying for a new house for a year. And I regularly sowed seed faith gifts to God through the Oral Roberts Ministries. I started with $5.75 and eventually moved up to $100. And then I added $66 more every month. I want you to know that this month, I'm moving into my new house!

Geraldine from Pennsylvania

Faithful Sowing and Praying Healed My Heart

I was diagnosed with cardiomyopathy, which is an enlarged heart. Only one-third of my heart muscle worked, and my heart was five centimeters larger than normal. My wife and I are seed faith partners with the Oral Roberts Ministries. And we've been sowing seed to God every month through your ministry. When I was diagnosed, the doctor said there was nothing they could do to help me. But I reminded God I've been sowing seed. My wife and I also called the Abundant Life Prayer Group for prayer. Since then, my heart has become smaller, and now it is back to normal size. My doctor is amazed! He said, "I have never seen anything like it in all the years that I have practiced medicine."

Rodger from Oklahoma

About the Author

Richard Roberts, B.A., M.A., D.Min., has dedicated his life to ministering the saving, healing, delivering power of Jesus Christ around the world. God has put a dream in Richard's heart of reaching the nations of the earth for Jesus. Since 1980, he has ministered God's healing power in 39 nations spanning six continents.

In his miracle healing outreaches, Richard has ministered to crowds of over 200,000 people in a single service. Often as much as half the audience responds for prayer to receive Jesus Christ as their personal Lord and Savior. Hundreds and thousands more receive healings and miracles as Richard ministers God's Word and operates in the gifts of the Holy Spirit, especially the word of knowledge.

Richard is the Chairman and CEO of Oral Roberts Evangelistic Association. He and his wife, Lindsay, host *The Place for Miracles* — a half-hour interactive broadcast that reaches out to millions worldwide. On this unique healing program, Richard ministers in the power of the Holy Spirit, praying for those who are sick or hurting in some area of their lives, and often giving specific words of knowledge about how God is touching people with His healing power. *The Place for Miracles* has received more than 148,000 phone calls to date from viewers who have reported miracles and answers to prayer.

Richard is a man on fire for God and consumed by the compassion of Jesus for sick and hurting people. His meetings across the United States and around the world are marked by a tremendous move of the Spirit, resulting in all types of physical, mental, emotional, financial, and spiritual healings. Richard says, "Jesus was born to step into a world of trouble and bring healing and deliverance, and that's the call of God upon my own life — to reach out to people in their troubles and heartaches, to pray and believe God, and to bring them His Word of hope and healing."

In addition to his responsibilities at the Oral Roberts Evangelistic Association, Richard also served as President of Oral Roberts University for 15 years. Since 2010, he has offered the Richard Roberts School of Miracles to help equip Christians with practical, hands-on experience in applying God's Word and His healing power in their own lives and in the lives of others, especially emphasizing how Christians can enjoy a life empowered by the Holy Spirit. To date, more than 35,000 students in 100 nations have studied these online courses. Richard has also authored a number of books, booklets, and other inspirational material, including *He's A Healing Jesus, When All Hell Breaks Loose, Claim Your Inheritance*, and his autobiography, *He's the God of a Second Chance.*

Richard and his wife, Lindsay, have three daughters: Jordan, Olivia, and Chloe.

RICHARD ROBERTS
ORAL ROBERTS MINISTRIES

Richard Roberts
P.O. Box 2187
Tulsa, OK 74102-2187

www.oralroberts.com

*For prayer anytime, call The Abundant Life Prayer Group at **918-495-7777**, or contact us online at **www.oralroberts.com/prayer.***